The Pa...
Meditations for when you hate your life

By Laura Baxter

Table of Contents

INTRODUCTION: Why Job?

There are so many things I wish I could say to my younger self, especially words of encouragement in suffering. I started my adulthood as an idealist, even moving to China and working at an orphanage. Since that time – 20 years ago now -- I have come to understand that pain is a large and inescapable part of life.

The great challenge for each human being is to find meaning in suffering. And if you believe in God, as I do, one of the most profound questions you can ask is, "Why would a good God allow suffering at all?" As I tried to process the pain in my own life, I eventually turned to the book of Job.

The Whole Story

Most people have some idea that the book of Job is about suffering. They may know that Job came under attack from Satan, and that after some time, God restored Job's health and fortunes. Riches to rags to riches: a tale quickly told. But that simple story is only 3 chapters, a picture frame. The great work of art consists in the other 39 chapters -- the poetic dialogue between Job, his four friends, and God.

So many times, we try to comfort ourselves with Sunday-school stories. And these are good as far as they go. I don't want to denigrate Sunday school. But God in His wisdom has given us the whole Bible, the whole book of Job, for our study, and meditation, and enlightenment.

We live in the age of Instagram. I have an Art Journaling Bible, and I love it. The margins are doodled with quick quotes, perfect for sharing on space-limited social media platforms. But these should only whet our appetites for the full text. You can eat a couple croutons, and call it salad, but your body knows the difference.

If I believe the Bible is the inspired word of God (and I do), I need to live like it. My soul needs me to tuck into the full text of the Scriptures. Vague Christian affirmations devoid of context will not strengthen me for the next trial. And the next trial is coming.

We must feast on the full banquet of God's word. We need the book of Job, all of it.

Journey of Faith

Sometimes Job and his friends say strange and uncomfortable things. Certainly many passages – beginning with Job's death-wish in chapter 3 – are quite depressing. And such passages go on, and on, and on. Yet in the darkest chapters of Job, and the darkest chapters of my life, God is faithful. He continues to unfold his words to us, bringing light (Psalm 119:130).

I began my odyssey through Job as a step of faith: faith in the fruitfulness of God's word, faith in the heart-prompts of the Holy Spirit. I have marinated in the book's beautiful poetry, marveled at Job's boldness, recoiled at the harshness of Job's so-called friends. And as Job draws my heart closer to the gospel, I cast out my line in hopes others may follow.

I have done my best to treat the text respectfully, for this is sacred ground. My practice is to read through several different translations and commentaries, pray, and then write. But I can't digest God's word for you. That would be gross. You must engage with your Bible directly, and allow the Holy Spirit to speak to your own heart.

To get the most out of this book, I encourage you to get a Bible in a translation you like. Prayerfully read each section, before reading any of my thoughts. Then go back and read your Bible again. In my experience, the possible insights from the book of Job are endless. Ask God to make the text come alive just for you.

If you have questions at any point, reach out to your pastor or small group. You can also contact me through my website at stirfrylaura.wordpress.com.

Job 1:1-12 (The Beginning)

Our story begins: "There was a man in the land of Uz whose name was Job." (v. 1).

There are no explicit markers indicating the time period when Job lived. There is no mention of Jewish history at all: no law of Moses, no Davidic dynasty, no exile in Babylon. The consensus of evangelical scholars appears to be that Job lived before those events. He lived in the ancient time of the Patriarchs. Although Job may have been unfamiliar with Jewish religious ceremony, he clearly served the one true God.

Along those lines, Job is noteworthy because of his integrity. He is "blameless and upright, one who feared God and turned away from evil." (v. 1). Job had a large family, 7 sons and 3 daughters. He worried that his children might secretly sin against God, so he continually interceded with God on their behalf. (v.2, 5).

Job is also noteworthy because of his wealth: 7 thousand sheep, 3 thousand camels, 500 yoke of oxen, 500 female donkeys, and lots of servants. These numbers are obvious approximations meant to impress the reader with a picture of vast and well-rounded riches. Job was "the greatest of all the people of the east." (v. 3).

And now the scene switches dramatically. We move from Job's human existence in Uz, to the unseen, spiritual realm. God is having a council meeting with the "sons of God," a divine audience of created spirit beings. There are different ancient words for spirit beings, but for convenience we might call these beings "angels." (v. 6).

Among the angels at this meeting we find a being named "Satan." We do not know if this was the same Satan or devil that tempted Christ in the New Testament. Nonetheless, this Satan shares the same malevolent, accusing characteristics. Satan has just come back from roaming the earth, a creepy occupation. (v. 6-7).

God asks Satan, "Have you considered my servant Job?" *Look what a great guy Job is. He is blameless and upright, he fears me and turns away from evil.* (v. 8). God is bragging on Job! He notices Job, he is happy about Job, he loves Job. We might think, what a great honor for Job to be mentioned this way at the divine council meeting. But the conversation does not stop there.

Satan challenges God's assessment of the situation. "Does Job fear God for no reason?" *Look at all the stuff you have given Job. He only loves you for the stuff. If you take the stuff away, Job will curse you to your face.* (v. 9-11). Satan is making a terrible accusation. God is pleased with Job, and Satan is trying to undermine that pleasure.

So what does God do? God allows the challenge to go forward. God gives Satan authority to destroy everything Job has. (v. 12). Unlike Satan, God does not predict the outcome one way or the other. In one sense (although God, of course, knows everything), God is taking a great risk. If Job loses everything, will he remain faithful? Or will God's pleasure with Job be proved hollow, as Satan has predicted?

Everything was going so well for Job. Why would God do this? This is one of the central questions of the book of Job. Why does God allow Job to suffer?

Job 1:13-22 (Disaster Strikes)

Picking up the story, we see God give Satan authority to destroy everything Job has, with one caveat: Do not touch Job himself. (v. 12). Satan is eager to execute all kinds of dark plans against Job, yet he can do nothing without God's permission. Where God says stop, Satan must stop. Still, Satan has enough latitude to get started. He leaves God's presence and hustles back to earth.

Meanwhile, Job's family continues to enjoy the good life, oblivious to Satan's schemes. We know from earlier in the chapter that Job's seven sons liked to take turns hosting family gatherings. On this particular day, everyone is at the home of Job's oldest son, eating and partying and drinking adult beverages. (v. 13).

It's so easy to assume that life will continue the way it always has. People were eating and drinking in the time of Noah, right before the flood destroyed the earth (Matthew 24:38). In one of Christ's parables, the Rich Fool expected to eat and drink for many years to come, yet he died that same night (Luke 12:19). Our human sight is limited. We don't know what discussions are taking place in God's divine council, we don't know what tomorrow will bring. Yet we do know that nothing happens outside God's control.

While Job's children are eating and drinking, four disasters fall in rapid succession. First, the Sabeans attack Job's oxen and donkeys, capturing the animals and killing the herdsmen. Second, "the fire of God" falls from heaven and burns up Job's massive flocks of sheep, along with the shepherds. Third, Chaldean raiders capture all Job's camels and kill those servants as well. Fourth, and most tragically, a great wind from the wilderness collapses the home of Job's oldest son, killing all the young family members inside. (vv. 13-19).

Satan, using God's delegated authority, has commandeered human, natural and supernatural elements to bring destruction on Job. Two of the disasters involve hostile tribesmen, from two separate regions. One disaster falls straight from heaven, the "fire of God." And the final disaster blows from the wilderness, an area associated with wandering evil spirits. All these very different elements bend to the decisions made in God's divine council. The Sabeans and Chaldeans were serving unseen forces just as surely as they were serving their own greed and lust for violence.

In the face of total calamity, Job "arose and tore his robe and shaved his head and fell on the ground." (v. 20). We can understand these bodily expressions of grief. But Job's final response is astonishing – Job worships God. Job says "Naked I came from my mother's womb, and naked shall I return. The Lord gave, and the Lord has taken away; blessed be the name of the Lord." (v. 21). Job did not honor God only for the stuff. Job did not presume upon the Lord's goodness. Instead, Job proclaimed God's sovereignty to do as he pleases.

The Bible tells us "In all this Job did not sin or charge God with wrong." (v. 22). Satan's prediction – that Job would curse God to his face – did not come true. Instead, Job blesses God.

And yet, Satan is not satisfied.

Job 2 (More Disaster)

So the divine council meets again, and Satan shows up again. Again the Lord brags on Job: *Blameless. Upright. Fears God. Turns from Evil.* God tells Satan, "Job still holds fast his integrity, although you incited me against him to destroy him without reason." (vv. 1-3). Satan's accusations against Job were baseless. Satan's destruction of Job's world was senseless. Yet mysteriously, God claims responsibility for granting Satan's request and giving him power over Job.

Then Satan doubles down on evil. "Skin for skin!" *Job still has his health. Take that away, strike his body with illness. Then he will curse you to his face.* For a second time, God meets the challenge. God gives Satan power over Job's body, yet he also commands Satan to spare Job's life. *Satan, you may go so far, and no more.* (vv. 4-6).

Satan takes what he can get. You can almost see Satan licking his chops, thinking up more ways to torment Job. He decides to inflict Job with foul sores, from the soles of his feet to the crown of his head. Not one part of Job's body is left untouched. Job sits in the ashes, trying to get some relief by scraping himself with a piece of broken pottery. But there is no relief. (vv. 7-8).

For the first time, we see Job's wife. She has also lost everything. She is also deeply grieving. But in her grief she adds to Job's test. Unwittingly, she mimics the words of Satan: "Do you still hold fast your integrity? Curse God and die!" You can almost hear Satan egging her on. (v. 9).

But Job's integrity is the only thing he has left. Job calls out his wife's error. *Don't speak like a foolish woman. You know better than that.* He says, "Shall we receive good from God, and shall we not receive evil?" Job acknowledges that God is sovereign over giving and taking. Job has no sense of entitlement, he understands

God owes him nothing. And so the text declares, "In all this Job did not sin with his lips." (v. 10).

Meanwhile, news of Job's misfortune travels. Three friends come from three different regions to visit: Eliphaz the Temanite, Bildad the Shuhite, and Zophar the Naamathite. They intend to show Job sympathy and comfort him. (v. 11). But when they arrive, Job is so disfigured that they do not recognize him. (v. 12). This small detail foreshadows the suffering servant of Isaiah, whose appearance was marred beyond human recognition (Isaiah 52:14). In the midst of overwhelming evil, we find a hint of something sacred.

Job's friends show him a lot of sympathy. They cry for Job, tear their robes, and toss dust on their heads. They sit on the ground with Job for an entire week, stunned into silence by Job's great suffering. (v. 13). In times of terrible grief, we need friends like that. Friends who comfort by just being there. Friends who don't try to stuff down sadness with more words.

Interlude: Gratitude and Skin Disease

You may be familiar with the story of the 10 lepers, from Luke chapter 17. Leprosy is a loathsome skin disease, and these 10 individuals were social outcasts. Yet they were bold enough to cry out to Jesus, "Master, have mercy on us!" Jesus indeed had mercy on them. He sent them on their way to the priests, and as they went they were healed. (Luke 17: 12-14). But this is only the backdrop for the real story.

One of the 10 lepers, after realizing that he was healed – no more loathsome skin disease! – "turned back, praising God with a loud voice; and he fell on his face at Jesus' feet, giving him thanks." This #tenpercent leper also happened to be from an outcast ethnic group, the Samaritans. Jesus, after commenting on the nine who did not return to praise God, told the one, "Rise and go your way; your faith has made you well." (Luke 17:16-19).

It's easy to see the lesson here – be sure to thank God for his blessings! I'm sure the 9 lepers were extremely happy to be healed, ecstatic even. But only one of them thought to treasure the healer. God gives us good gifts all the time. He did not spare his own Son! He promises to give us the world! (Romans 8:32). But all these gifts are intended to point us to the Giver, to increase our love and praise for the Lord rather than the blessings themselves.

So what does this have to do with Job? When we first meet Job, he does not receive blessings from God. Instead, all of his wealth and all of his children are destroyed. Rather than be healed of a loathsome skin disease, Job was inflicted with a loathsome skin disease. And listen to what Job did: "Job... fell on the ground and worshiped. And he said, 'Naked I came from my mother's womb, and naked shall I return. The Lord gave, and the Lord has taken away, blessed by the name of the Lord." (1:20-21) Later, when Job's wife tells him to curse God and die, Job rebukes her saying, "Shall we receive good from God, and shall we not receive evil?" (2:10)

This is the posture of the believer, on the ground, at the feet of Jesus, worshiping and giving thanks. Whether God gives the loathsome skin disease or miraculously takes it away, God also provides the power to give thanks in all circumstances.

But Job's story does not end with the loathsome skin disease. It goes on for another 42 chapters. The disastrous opening turns to lament after dark lament. Job accuses God of injustice and demands an audience. Yet what Job missed most was God's presence with him. Satan had accused Job of using God, of serving God only for his blessings. But in the raw anguish of Job's cries, we find that he truly did love the Giver more.

In his pain, Job wrongly saw the withdrawal of God's blessings as the withdrawal of God's favor. But - SPOILER ALERT -- this was only a season in Job's long life. Fortunately, like the story of the leper, the story of Job has a happy ending. Out of the whirlwind, God answered Job's cry. Job got to experience God up close and personal, to see God with his own eyes (42:5). Job is restored, he is comforted, and even his good fortune returns to him.

As long as we continue on earth, our stories are not yet done. God gives blessings and God gives pain, all for our good and his glory (Romans 8:28). Will we run to the Giver in good times and bad? Will we fall at his feet and worship for the gift of his presence alone? For this is how Satan is defeated, both now and in eternity.

Job 3 (A Death-Wish)

For a week Job sits with his three friends in silence. Then Job finally opens his mouth – to curse the day he was born. *May darkness, gloom, clouds and blackness mark my birthday.* Job's intense suffering taints how he views his own life story. He turns a happy event into something sinister. "Why did I not die at birth?" Job asks. He releases his grief in a hauntingly raw poem. (vv. 3-19).

From the text, we know Job is a righteous man. At the same time, pain can make the faithful believer forget important truths. God formed Job in his mother's womb, with great care and design. God also formed Job's life history. Job is right not to curse God, but he is wrong to curse God's handiwork. This is a dark chapter for Job. He has forgotten that with God, night is as bright as day. (Psalm 139:11-16).

Job continues: "Why is light given to him who is in misery?" (v. 20). *What is the purpose of my life of suffering?* It's funny how when things go well, we don't ask why. We don't wonder about our purpose, we don't think about death. But sooner or later, we will all suffer. And then the question comes: Why?

This is a good and important question. All religions, all life philosophies must grapple with the question of why people suffer. Spoiler alert: there are no pat answers. But as we struggle along with Job, we gradually uncover layers of truth.

Job's thoughts turn darker. He longs for death. *At least death is quiet, peaceful. At least then I can sleep, I won't be tormented by these horrible sores. I won't be tormented by my memories.* (v. 13). Indeed, death is the great equalizer: "The small and the great are there, and the slave is free from his master." To Job's suffering eyes, death is better than life. Job sees rest and a kind of resolution in death.

In the book of Ecclesiastes, King Solomon also questioned the meaning of life. Like Job, Solomon flirted with the idea that death is better than life. But he ultimately concluded that where there is life, there is hope (Ecclesiastes 9:4). We will see that there is still hope for Job.

What about Job's desire for rest from his torment? The New Testament declares that, if our only rest is in death, our faith is pathetic. We find our rest not in death, but in the life of Christ (Matthew 11:28, Hebrews 4:9). Christ has triumphed over the grave (I Corinthians 15:19, 55).

At the moment, these mysteries are veiled to Job. And yet we continue to see hints of the gospel. Job's sighs replace his food, and his groans pour out like water. Job's lament echoes the laments we find in the Psalms, especially Psalms 22, 42, and 88. These Psalms, in turn, foreshadow the sufferings of Jesus. Our savior knows, really knows, what suffering is like. His presence goes with us as we suffer.

There are times when we rejoice and wonder at God's closeness (Psalm 139:5-6). But to Job, in his time of pain, God's presence feels oppressive. *God has hedged me in.* Job says, "The thing I fear comes upon me, and what I dread befalls me." What does Job fear and dread? The text tells us that Job fears *God.* (Job 31:23).

God has ultimate power and sovereignty. Sometimes this thought is comforting, and sometimes it is terrifying. God is not tame, he is not an emotional support animal.

Job 4 (Whose Fault Is It?)

What do you say to a friend who is hurting so much, he wants to die? Eliphaz jumps right in. He can't help himself. *Job, you're the one who fears God, right? You're the one who holds on to his integrity, right? You talked a good talk, you helped a lot of people. But when disaster comes to you, you get discouraged. I think it's time for a dose of your own medicine!* (vv. 1-6).

Everyone knew Job as a man of good character, a moral leader. Eliphaz used to look up to Job. When Job's misfortune first hit, Eliphaz traveled out to visit and mourned with Job for a week. But now Job's suffering is dragging on, and Eliphaz is doubting his prior opinions. Shouldn't Job, of all people, know how to handle adversity? In fact, why would a guy like Job suffer adversity at all? Does he have some secret sin?

When other people suffer, we jump to blame: it must be their own fault. Eliphaz states, "As I have seen, those who plow iniquity and sow trouble reap the same." (v. 8). We take weird comfort from telling ourselves, "This person just made bad choices." Subconsciously we think, "As long as I avoid those choices, that bad thing won't happen to me." We focus on the experiential world of cause and effect, where human actions lead to results that, while painful, seem to make sense.

But the Bible teaches a more complex narrative. Of course, we often act foolishly and suffer the consequences. But other times, good people suffer through no fault of their own. The text clearly tells us that Job is righteous. He is not suffering due to some secret sin, but because his righteousness drew the attention of heaven!

In the New Testament, Jesus' own disciples fell into the thinking of Eliphaz. They saw a man born blind, and asked "Who sinned, this man or his parents?" Jesus responded, "Neither. This suffering happened that the works of God might be displayed in him." (John

9:2-3). Suffering can be redeemed, transformed. It can display the works of God.

Jesus himself was mocked and doubted when he hung on the cross. "He saved others; he cannot save himself... He trusted in God; let God deliver him now, if he desires him." (Matthew 27:42-43). Yet we know Jesus was righteous, more righteous than Job. And Jesus' great suffering was God's greatest work in history.

Returning to our story, Eliphaz describes a strange night vision. "A spirit glided past my face; the hair of my flesh stood up." Eliphaz is filled with dread as the spirit speaks. *Mortal man can never be right before God. God sets a high standard for his divine servants. How can humans in their mud huts measure up? Humans die an ignorant death, and nobody cares, least of all God.* (v. 12-21).

It is true that, outside of Christ, no human is pure before God. Not even Job. At the same time, the Bible is clear that God watches over us with care and compassion. And although humans are "a little lower than the heavenly beings," yet God has given mankind authority to rule over the earth that he created (Psalm 8). In fact, some day God's people will even judge spiritual beings, perhaps including the spirit that visited Eliphaz (I Corinthians 6:3).

We know Satan initiated the attack on Job. An accusing spirit heaps on more condemnation, through Eliphaz. It is an odd thought, but perhaps Satan and his spirits are jealous of the relationship God has with Job.

But can that relationship endure under the pressure of Job's pain?

Job 5 (Truth Can Be Annoying)

After describing his vision of the mocking spirit, Eliphaz continues: *Don't bother calling on angels for help. The life of a fool is full of aggravation. If your children are crushed, if your wealth is stolen, there's a good chance you are living foolishly. Trouble doesn't just spring up out of nowhere.* According to Eliphaz, "man is born to trouble as the sparks fly upward." (vv. 1-7). If Job has trouble, he can only blame himself.

These callous statements provide no comfort to Job. For sure, sometimes we can trace our troubles to foolish behavior. But many miserable situations (like Job's) cannot be explained by poor choices.

Then Eliphaz switches gears. He assumes an air of piety. "As for me, I would seek God, and to God would I commit my cause." *God is great, God is good. Let us thank him for our food.* According to Eliphaz, God cares for the poor and lowly, but "He catches the wise in their own craftiness, and the schemes of the wily are brought to a quick end." *God is a God of justice. He saves the needy from the hand of the mighty.* (vv. 8-16).

We know these things are all true. God is the source of all good gifts. He causes the proud to stumble, and he loves to lift up the humble. As the virgin Mary sang, God "has brought down the mighty from their thrones and exalted those of humble estate; he has filled the hungry with good things, and the rich he has sent away empty." (Luke 1:52-53.) But Eliphaz is no shining example of humility. Can Job accept the precious truth in these words, from a "friend" who has falsely accused him?

Eliphaz goes on to encourage Job, "Blessed is the one whom God reproves; therefore despise not the discipline of the Almighty." *God has wounded you, but he will also heal you.* (vv. 17-19). This is easy for Eliphaz to say, since he is not the one undergoing discipline. And yet, we know that Eliphaz is again speaking truth. Many times, the Bible tells us that God disciplines us faithfully, in love, like a good father disciplines his children.

Surprisingly, Eliphaz then prophesies blessings over Job. *God has promised to save you from famine, from war, and even from "the lash of the tongue."* [Does that include tongue-lashings from Job's so-called friends?] *Job, you will be at peace at home and in the field. Before you die at a ripe old age, you will see many descendants.* (vv. 20-27). That's very nice for Eliphaz to say. But how can Eliphaz be so confident about this?

Eliphaz has an attitude of superiority that just grates. Job's life is in shambles, and Eliphaz blames Job. Eliphaz reminds Job that God is good, and tells Job to appreciate God's discipline. Then, Eliphaz confidently prophesies that everything will be OK. "Know it for your good," he says (v. 27). What an annoying guy!

Yet there are timeless truths in Eliphaz's words. Job needs to hear about God's goodness. Job needs to be reminded that discipline has a purpose. Job especially needs to trust in God's promises for his future.

As friends, do we express truth with compassion, so that those who suffer are able to hear it?

As sufferers, do we accept the truth that can heal us, despite the flaws of the messenger?

Job 6 (Kindness vs. Fear)

Eliphaz has just served Job a platter of platitudes, a mixture of truth and condescension. Job responds: *You can't understand what I am going through. Maybe my words have been a little rash, but you try bearing grief this heavy* - "heavier than the sand of the sea." *I have been hit by poison arrows from God, and it is terrifying.* (vv. 2-4).

Job admits he has been something of a jackass - "Does a wild donkey bray when he has grass?" (v. 5). When there is lots of fresh green food around, even a donkey is quiet. But Job has a gnawing pit of hunger in his soul. Job sees nothing filling, nothing refreshing, only tasteless mush that turns his stomach. (v. 6-7). Perhaps this is a metaphor for the advice from his friends!

Continuing his donkey-like braying from chapter 3, Job claims he still wants to die. He begs God to crush him and cut him off. (v. 8-9). Certainly Satan would get a kick out of killing Job in some brutal fashion. Yet this is the exact request denied by God – God specifically told Satan to spare Job's life. In contrast, we know God did not spare the life of his own son. Jesus was crushed and cut off so that we might be healed. (Isaiah 53). So sometimes suffering does end in death, and even death can glorify God. But this is not the path God has set for Job.

Job comforts himself with the thought, "I have not denied the words of the Holy One." At the same time, he wonders how long he can hold out. "Is my strength the strength of stones, or is my flesh bronze? Have I any help in me, when resource is driven from me?" (vv. 10-13). Job admits that he is weak and helpless. Human will power can only take us so far. Yet we know our savior is mighty; he does have the strength of stones and flesh of bronze (Ezekiel 1:27). When will Job's salvation come?

Meanwhile, Job starts to complain about his friends. "He who withholds kindness from a friend forsakes the fear of the Almighty."

He compares his friends to a flash flood of treacherous, icy waters. Yet when he looks for refreshment, the streams have melted back into the wasteland. Job's hope for comfort has vanished like a mirage. (vv. 14-20).

What is going on with Job's friends? Job didn't ask them for money, he didn't expect them to solve his problems. All he wanted was a little kindness during his time of trouble. According to Job, "you see my calamity and are afraid." (v. 21). Do they think Job's condition is contagious?

Job tells his friends "the speech of a despairing man is wind." *Don't take my words at face value. I just don't understand what has happened to me. Don't criticize me, help me make sense of this.* He accuses his friends of "casting lots" and "bargaining" over him in his suffering. *I am more than just an interesting object lesson for your discussion.* (vv. 24-27).

Then Job pleads, "Look at me! Please turn toward me!" *Don't distance yourself from me. See me for who I really am. You have to believe me when I say that I am innocent!* (vv. 28-30). Job's strength is crumbling. His friends have failed him. He continues to fantasize about death.

When others suffer, do we respond in fear? Do we judge from a distance, criticizing the rash words of desperate people?

How can we show kindness and give refreshment, instead? How can we look with eyes that see the precious human being behind the suffering?

Job 7 (Worms in Dirt)

Job continues his lament. He compares himself to a hired hand, engaged in difficult manual labor. But instead of work, Job is assigned "months of emptiness" and "nights of misery." At least the laborer can rest in the shade when his duties are done. But Job cannot rest – he tosses and turns. (vv. 1-4).

"My flesh is clothed with worms and dirt," says Job. His body is disgusting and decaying. Job watches his days -- relentlessly heading toward The Big End – and he sees no hope. *My life is a breath. I will never see good things again. I will vanish before your eyes, I will be gone and forgotten forever.* (vv. 5-10).

As the Teacher of Ecclesiastes reminds us, "All are from the dust, and to dust all return." Dust to dust, ashes to ashes. When hope is gone, we cling to the dirt, we become like worms (Psalm 119:25; Psalm 22:6). We came from the wormy dirt, and that is where we will return some day. Job sees this reality on his own putrid skin.

Yes, Job will die some day. But will he never see good things again? Is it true that those who go down to the grave do not come back up? Will Job be forgotten forever? No, no and no! Job will see good things, he will see his Redeemer after the grave, he will not be forgotten. In fact, if Job could look thousands of years into the future, he would see readers and authors and preachers and bloggers drawing wisdom and comfort from his story.

Job's rash words come from the anguish of his spirit, the bitterness of his soul. His pain colors his views of life, death and even God. Most of us draw comfort from the thought of God guarding our bed at night. But to Job, God's watchful eye has become a terrifying nightmare. *God, leave me alone! Let me die!*

The Psalmist sees God's care as marvelous, miraculous: "When I look at your heavens, the work of your fingers, the moon and the stars, which you have set in place, what is man that you are mindful of him, and the son of man that you care for him?" (Psalm 8:3-4). Yet for Job, this care is suffocating. "What is man, that you make so much of him, and that you set your heart on him, visit him every morning and test him every moment?" *God, leave me alone! Stop watching me!* (vv. 17-20).

But God is not like Job's friends. God continues to watch Job and does not leave him alone.

Job continues his rant against God. *Why are you targeting me? Why am I such a burden to you?* (v. 20). In our suffering we often ask, "If God loves me, why did this bad thing happen?" Author Nancy Guthrie suggests a better question: <u>Because</u> God loves me, why – for what purpose - did this bad thing happen? Not "<u>if</u> God loves me," but "<u>because</u> God loves me." We are still under God's watchful care, even when bad things happen. And God promises to turn all bad things to good, for those who love him.

Job goes on to voice the biggest why: *Why don't you take away the stain on my soul?* (v. 21). Although Job is a righteous man, under the blinding light of the gaze of God, he feels his sin. As Peter said to Christ, "Depart from me, for I am a sinful man." (Luke 5:8). Yet Jesus did not leave Peter, and God does not leave Job. Thank God that our prayers to be left alone are not granted.

Job looks forward to death, where he thinks God will not find him. But we know from the Psalmist, "If I make my bed in the grave, you are there!" (Psalm 139:8). Though Job is a worm in the dirt, God sees and has not forgotten.

Job 8 (Truth without Love)

Job has just finished his second, melancholy monologue.
Impatient, Bildad the Shuhite jumps in, calls Job a windbag. *How
long will you go on like this, Job?* (v. 2).

Note that Job has already admitted "the speech of a despairing
man is wind." (6:26). So you would think Bildad would cut Job
some slack. But no. Along with Eliphaz, Bildad continues the
practice of taking God's truth and beating Job over the head with it.

God is just, he can do no wrong. [No duh, thinks Job.] *So your
children must have sinned against him, and he allowed them to
experience the consequences.* [Ouch, not helpful, thinks Job.]
Seek God and ask him for mercy [What do you think I've been
doing? thinks Job.] *If you are righteous, God will come down and
help you.* [I am as righteous as I know how to be, but God hasn't
helped me at all. Instead, God sent YOU, thinks Job.]

Then Bildad prophesies over Job: "... though your beginning
was small, your latter days will be very great." (v. 7). This echoes
the earlier prophecy of Eliphaz, that Job will be delivered, again
have many offspring, and live to a ripe old age (Job 5:19-27).
Somehow, these two terrible comforters have spoken words that –
SPOILER ALERT – actually come true.

Bildad goes on. *I'm not just speaking for myself. Sure, in the
grand scheme of things, we were born yesterday, we know nothing.
But our ancestors have searched out such questions, and we can
learn from their wisdom.* (vv. 9-10).

Certainly, we are talking about a timeless question: Why would
a good God allow bad things to happen? Others have pondered
these issues before us, and we should learn everything we can from
their experience. But is Bildad's reliance on tradition any better
than the creepy vision of Eliphaz?

According to Bildad, the ancient elders believed in cause-and-
effect – no surprise there. *When the river dries up, the reeds wither*

and die. God is the source of life, and those who forget him will likewise perish. Without God, your confidence will break apart like spider webs. Sure, you may start life with a growth spurt, like a plant in the sun, but soon you will be destroyed with no one to remember. "God will not reject a blameless man, nor take the hand of evildoers." (vv. 11-20).

Then, perhaps feeling he has been too harsh on poor Job, Bildad ends on a more positive note: *If you are truly blameless, there is hope. You will see laughter again, and your enemies will be put to shame.* (v. 20-22).

For the second time, we see a would-be comforter, speaking words of truth and even encouragement. Bildad gives an interesting intellectual discourse, including the perspective of ancient fathers. Yet these words miss the mark and bring no relief to Job. We see very little love or compassion from Bildad.

As the Apostle Paul says, "If I have prophetic powers, and understand all mysteries and all knowledge [and what knowledge is greater than the knowledge of why we suffer?] ... but have not love, I am nothing."

May God help us share both truth and love with those who suffer.

Job 9 (Awesome God Against Me)

Bildad has joined Eliphaz in repeating old formulas: We know God blesses the righteous and curses the wicked. Therefore, if you are suffering, you must have done something wrong.

I know all your formulas! says Job. *But how can a mere mortal please God?* Perhaps Job is thinking of all his previous efforts, including prayers and sacrifices for his now-dead children. If Job of all people is punished by God, how can anyone be truly righteous? Job imagines a celestial lawsuit, *Almighty God of the Universe vs. Poor Sick Job.* (v. 3). How could the scales of justice ever tip in Job's favor?

Job is a great poet, and he transitions into an amazing tribute to God's majesty. *The Lord is wise in heart and mighty in strength. God doesn't just move mountains – he shakes the earth to its roots. He stops the sun from rising, stops the stars from twinkling. God stretched out the sky and trampled over the stormy sea.* (vv. 4-8). Echoing Eliphaz in 5:9, Job agrees that God "does great things beyond searching out, and marvelous things beyond number." Job even uses mythological imagery, describing the henchmen of the primordial sea monster bowing beneath God's feet (v. 13). In a rap battle about the awesomeness of God, Job would beat his friends every time.

God's handiwork is obvious to Job, but he doesn't see God's presence. *God has passed me by, he has moved on, no one will turn him back. And God is angry with me.* (vv. 11-13).

I'm a good guy, says Job. *But what can I say to Almighty God?* In a human court of law, the parties can serve each other with various interrogatories and requests for information, all of which must be answered under oath. But Job can't think what he would answer to God. Job certainly can't believe God would answer him. All Job can do is appeal for mercy. (vv. 14-16).

Job thinks about how God has crushed him, how God has multiplied his wounds "without cause." Job doesn't see any way out of his situation. Filled with bitterness, Job hates his life. (vv. 17-21). In this foul frame of mind, Job begins to doubt God's goodness. And here, the righteous Job speaks in error:

God destroys both the blameless and the wicked. God sadistically mocks the pain of the innocent. God covers the face of justice so that the wicked inherit the earth. If it is not God, then who? (vv. 22-24).

Job turns back to his own situation. *The days of my life run away like an errand-boy, they float by like a reed boat, they fly off like a swooping eagle. I try to put on a smile and pretend nothing is wrong. But my mask crumbles, and I cannot jolly myself out of my pain. I am condemned before God. If I wash myself with snow, or scrub my hands raw with lye, God himself will throw me in a slimy pit.* (vv. 25-31).

God is altogether alien from me – how can I speak to him, much less face him in some heavenly courthouse? Oh how I wish for a mediator to stand between us, with one hand on each of our shoulders. Someone to take away God's punishing rod, so that I am no longer terrified. If I had that, I could speak to God with confidence. (vv. 32-35).

We feel Job's pain, just as we feel our own pain in various trials. But we don't have to despair with Job. The good news is that God is awesome, and God is <u>not</u> against us. In fact, God sent his Son to bridge the infinite gap between his holiness and our sin. Christ was crushed, and wounded, and mocked, so that we could be healed and cleansed. With Jesus as our mediator, we can approach God's throne with confidence (Hebrews 4:14-16). Hang in there, Job!

Interlude: Two Patriarchs Who Hate Their Life

Who would you rather be, the guy who has everything – or the guy who lost everything?

Exhibit A is our friend Job: children dead, wealth stolen, and body stricken with a loathsome skin disease. Exhibit B, just a few books later, is the Preacher-King of Ecclesiastes: insanely smart, massively rich, and living a life of exquisite pleasure.

You can understand Job saying, "I hate my life." (Job 9: 21). But why would the Preacher say the same thing? "So I hated life, because what is done under the sun was grievous to me, for all is vanity and a striving after the wind." (Ecc. 2:17). Why would super-success push someone to the same conclusions as bitter suffering?

The author of Proverbs asks God to "give me neither poverty nor riches." (Proverbs 30:9). As I grow older, I have come to appreciate "boring" more and more. The line between pleasure and pain is quite thin. There is something to be said for a simple, quiet life: working with your hands, loving your family and neighbors, accepting your lot with contentment (Ecclesiastes 5:18-20; I Thessalonians 4:9-12; 1 Timothy 6:6-8). Even on a larger scale, a robust middle class marks a healthy society; a nation split between rich and poor balances precariously on the brink of disaster.

But we can't expect to live life always in the "sweet spot." Both Job and the Preacher-King recognize that the world is not as it should be. Job suffers despite a life of righteousness. The Preacher fears his legacy will be turned over to a fool, and ultimately forgotten (Ecc. 2:16, 21). Both men observe that righteous and wicked, wise and fool, all enter the grave together

(Ecc. 2:16, Job 21:23-26). Both men wonder, implicitly and explicitly, what benefit comes from right living? (Ecc. 3:10, Job 34:9).

Faced with this crisis of meaning, the Preacher steps back and coldly analyzes the world, from a distance. He notes the repeating patterns of nature: the circuit of the sun, the currents of the wind, the cycle of water rushing to the seas (Ecc. 1:5-7). It's a picture of a mechanistic world, on auto-play. Like the physical world, humans also pass through various life phases: birth, death, building, destroying, tears, laughter, silence, speaking, even war and peace (Ecc. 3:1-8). There is a "time for everything," and it all feels very impersonal.

In contrast, Job's suffering has made the crooked world extremely personal. Job doesn't deal in abstractions, doesn't say, "oh well, there's a time for everything and it's my time to be poor and sick." Job cries to God in a very direct way: "Why are you acting as my enemy? Show yourself, and answer me!" (Job chs. 9, 31).

Both Job and the Preacher eventually return to God, for the meaning of life is found in God alone. The Preacher reaches his destination after a lifetime of weary study: "The end of the matter; all has been heard." (Ecc. 12:12-13). To his readers, the Preacher warns, "Remember also your Creator in the days of your youth... Fear God and keep his commandments, for this is the whole duty of man." (Ecc. 12:1, 13). But even here, in the frailty of old age, with death at his doorstep, the Preacher remains detached.

In contrast, Job's return to God is, again, extremely personal. God appears in a whirlwind, reveals mysteries without wearisome study. Yes, the universe is planned, but it is also a delight. It reflects a Personality, not simply mechanical rules. The sea is a big baby with a foggy diaper. The sunrise shakes the skirts of the earth. The thunder rings with God's battle cry, as he leads the stars in a heavenly parade. (Job ch. 38). Job responds, "I had heard of you by the hearing of the ear, but now my eye sees you," and he falls down in repentance (42:5-6). And the best days of Job's life are still to come.

Who would you rather be – the guy who has everything, or the guy who loses everything?

Job 10 (Stinky Cheese Man)

Psalm 139 is one of my favorite psalms. David begins, "O Lord, you have searched me and known me!" David is amazed at the nearness of God, and he rejoices in how God knows him intimately. David cannot escape God's presence, nor does he want to: "If I ascend to heaven, you are there! If I make my bed in the grave, you are there!" David marvels at how God knitted him together in his mother's womb. God planned David's path from birth to the end of his days. David longs to be even closer, to have God search and remove any evil from his thoughts.

And then we get to Job 10, the Anti-Psalm 139. "I HATE MY LIFE!" says Job (v. 1).

God, you formed me, you knit me together in my mother's womb. You are the Potter, the Weaver... the divine Cheese-Monger. Yes, Job compares his embryonic form to cheese doodles (v. 10). *So why did you make me just to destroy me? Why are you scrutinizing me, nit-picking me, hunting me down? You know I can't win against you!* (vv. 14-17).

I remember when your presence gave me life. I remember experiencing your love. I remember your care for me, my care for you. Was that previous life a lie? Were you planning to spring this on me all along? (v. 12).

Job accuses God of despising him and "favoring the designs of the wicked." (v. 3). According to Job, God has destroyed him "altogether." (v. 8). Job doesn't know that God is, in fact, protecting him. God specifically told Satan not to take Job's life. Satan may despise Job and take sadistic pleasure in Job's suffering. But God emphatically does not work that way. God afflicts us in faithfulness and love, for our good (Psalm 119:71, 75-76).

In verse 18, Job starts back up with "I wish I was dead" – the same song he was singing in Chapter 3. *Why was I born? I wish I had gone straight from womb to tomb.* "GOD, LEAVE ME ALONE!" (v. 20).

What a contrast between David and Job. To David, God's presence is a comforting blanket of protection. To Job, God's presence is suffocating. Job asks God for space, to find "a little cheer" before he leaves this world for good. Job imagines death as "the land of darkness and deep shadow, the land of gloom like thick darkness, like deep shadow without any order, where light is thick darkness." (vv. 21-22). Job predicts that the last light will wink into darkness. In fact, he looks forward to being absolutely anonymous.

But God provides a response in Psalm 139. "If I say, 'Surely the darkness shall cover me, and the light about me be night,' even the darkness is not dark to you; the night is bright as the day, for darkness is as light with you." For David, no darkness can conquer God's light. God sees into the deepest, darkest pit, and he brings us out. He is with us through the Valley of the Shadow of Death. Our lives do not end in death, darkness and anonymity; God will lead us in the "way everlasting."

How have you experienced God's presence? How can you move from Job 10 to Psalm 139?

Job 11 (Hee Haw)

Job finishes his death-wish monologue, and his third friend Zophar speaks. Although this is the first time we hear from Zophar, his themes are familiar.

Geez, Job, are you done talking yet? Blah blah yak yak, 'I'm an innocent man,' yadda yadda yadda. I wish God would speak up and answer you. God could give you the secrets of wisdom, but you're only looking at one side of things. God's wisdom is multi-faceted. In fact, if it wasn't for your tunnel vision, you would see God is treating you better than you deserve. (vv. 1-6).

Zophar, like the other so-called friends, thinks it is impossible for calamity to fall on a righteous person. Otherwise, the world becomes unpredictable, frightening. Certainly, Job cannot be as innocent as he claims. Job must have some secret sins.

In one sense Zophar is correct – we are all worse than we think. Even in our suffering, God is better to us than we deserve. But at the same time, Scripture tells us that Job was a righteous man. And while obedience to God promotes human flourishing, God doesn't work by formula. We can't manipulate God by our good works. Sometimes evil people prosper for mysterious reasons known only to God.

Cue Psalm 73. Asaph the song-writer maintains that God is good to those who are pure in heart. Yet when he looks around, he sees that evil people are doing pretty well: "always at ease, they increase in riches." (Psalm 73:12). Asaph thinks about all his efforts to do the right thing, and wonders if he is wasting his time.

As he meditates in the Holy Spirit, Asaph realizes that — whatever evil people may get from this life – he has God Himself. "Whom have I in heaven but you? And there is nothing on earth that I desire besides you. My flesh and my heart may fail, but God is the strength of my heart and my portion forever." (Psalm 73:25-26). Asaph also takes comfort in the fact that God will ensure justice in the end. As song-writer Sandra McCracken reminds us, "This is not okay, so I know this is not the end."

Back to Zophar, who waxes eloquent about the mysteries of God. *God has no limit. His mysteries are higher than heaven, deeper than the grave, longer than earth, wider than the ocean.* (vv. 7-9). We are reminded of Psalm 139, how God's presence stretches from heaven to "the uttermost parts of the sea." We are reminded of Ephesians 3:18-19, where Paul prays that believers may have strength to understand the breadth and length and height and depth of the love of Christ.

But Zophar turns the deep things of God into an insult: "A stupid man will get understanding when a wild donkey's colt is born a man!" (v. 12). *Job, you are a jackass, and it would take a miracle for you to understand what God is doing.*

Perhaps Zophar knows he has gone too far. Like Bildad in chapter 8, Zophar tries to end on a positive note. *Turn to God, stretch your hands to him, put away your sin. God will heal your loathsome sores, so you can lift your face without blemish. You will forget your misery, you will enjoy safety and security. In fact, your life will be brighter than the noonday!* (vv. 13-19).

It is always good advice to turn from sin and toward God. But we cannot expect immediate, material success as a result. Job is starting to understand that we cannot hope in our own righteousness (9:30-31). But in his depression, Job despairs of any hope other than death – a fate shared with the wicked. (v. 20). Hang in there, Job

Job 12 (World Turned Upside-Down)

Job is hurt by the lack of compassion, and the condescending attitudes, of his so-called friends. He begins his fourth monologue with sarcasm: *You guys think you are so smart. "Just trust God, Job, and it will all be OK." Who hasn't heard that piece of advice? Because you are comfortable, you look down on losers like me.* (vv. 1-5).

Things are not making sense to Job. Job was loyal to God, they had a relationship. Job thinks about the past, when God heard him and answered his prayers. And now Job has become a laughingstock. Meanwhile, "the tents of robbers are at peace, and those who provoke God are secure." (v. 6). The world seems upside-down.

Job continues: *The older we get, the more we realize.* (v. 12). *Just look at nature, the birds, the beasts, the fish, even the plants. Every life, including human life, is sustained by God. The whole world trembles in his hands.* (vv. 7-10). We know from the words of Christ that God cares for the sparrows and the lilies of the field (Matt. 6:25-29). But Job sees a darker side to God's power. What God created, he can also destroy.

God is surely wise and mighty. When he tears down, no one can rebuild. He controls the waters; both drought and flood are from his hand. He holds the deceiver and the deceived. All you who think you are wise -- counselors, judges, kings, priests, elders, princes – God will send you away stripped and ashamed. The God who brought light from darkness, order from chaos -- this same God destroys nations. He makes the chiefs of the people stagger blindly in the wilderness. (vv. 13-25).

Job recognizes God's awesome power over all things. We are right to fear God's power to destroy. Thunderstorms, earthquakes, and volcanoes demonstrate forces beyond our understanding. Nonetheless, Job's perspective is skewed. The wisdom of God has many sides (11:6). God raises the storm - and he also stills it. God dries out the land - and then he waters it. God causes affliction - and then he heals. He does all these things to demonstrate his steadfast love. Psalm 107, which has a great, extended meditation on the topic of how God sends both disaster and relief, all for the purpose of drawing us to himself in love.

Meanwhile, Psalm 104 tells us that God rules creation with great tenderness. He makes springs gush forth, so the wild donkeys can drink. He makes grass grow up, so the cows can eat. God provides the means for people to craft wine, and oil, and bread, so they can grow happy and strong. "These all look to you... when you open your hand, they are filled with good things." (Psalm 104:27-28). Even the sea monster Leviathan frolics under God's care (Psalm 104:26).

Back in Job 12, our long-suffering protagonist correctly notices how God often shames the self-righteous, the powerful, those who think they are wise. Pride goes before the fall. And yet again, there is another side to this phenomenon. After the fall, God does not abandon us. The Apostle Paul shares the rest of the story: "God chose what is foolish in the world to shame the wise; God chose what is weak in the world to shame the strong... so that no human being might boast in the presence of God." (I Cor. 1:27-29).

The world is upside-down, but not in the way Job thinks. God uses his power in the service of his tender care. God brings down the mighty from their thrones, and then he exalts the humble (Matt. 1:52-53). God will not break the bruised reed, he will not snuff out the flickering candle (Matthew 12:20). His care for Job may be veiled, but it is ever-present.

Job 13 (A Bold Request)

Job snaps back to the present. He turns on his friends: *Stop your condescending platitudes! I know the natural order of things as well as you do. But you have gone too far. Instead of healing the wounded, you add insult to injury. You have plastered over my life with lies, trying to make it fit your tidy worldview. Just shut up already!* (vv. 1-5).

God doesn't need you to explain Him. He doesn't need your help, your justifications. We know God hates biased arguments – that includes bias in His favor. You can't use deceit to suck up to God. You don't know Who you are trying to "help." The Lord will rebuke you, and you will know the terror of His majesty. All your fine talk is just dirt and ashes. (vv. 7-12).

Then Job takes the plunge. *I want to talk to God. Let me at Him already! I may be taking my life in my hands, but so be it. I want to argue to God's face.* "Though He slay me, I will hope in Him." (vv. 3, 13-15).

This is a bold move by Job. How will God respond? Job's friends don't challenge God like this. Yet they reduce God to a formula, and slander Job to make God seem more righteous. Job rejects the formula. He wants to talk to God face-to-face, even if it kills him. Job has hope that God is approachable, that it is somehow possible to dialogue with God.

We have seen this kind of boldness before, in the Patriarchs. Abraham argues with God – politely -- over the fate of the city of Sodom (Genesis 18). Jacob wrestles with God in human form until God blesses him (Genesis 32). Moses pleads with God over the fate of Israel (Exodus 32). In each of these cases, God was not offended at all. In fact, God seemed rather pleased, and responded favorably. (Although God did dislocate Jacob's hip.) In the New Testament, Jesus seemed to praise forcefulness in laying hold of the Kingdom of Heaven (Matthew 11:12), as well as impudent, persistent seeking (Luke 11).

Does God want us to take bold risks in seeking Him, in seeking answers from Him?

Job thinks he is in the right – that he did nothing to deserve his great suffering – and he is prepared to argue his case with God. However, Job also knows there are some barriers. For Job to speak with God, God will have to withdraw His hand of judgment (vv. 21-22). Otherwise, Job will be paralyzed with dread. Job remembers the sins of his youth, and Job suspects he may have other, unknown sins as well. God must voluntarily level the playing field.

"Make me know my transgression and my sin," says Job. *But then show Your face. Don't count me as Your enemy. Call to me, let me answer You. Don't leave me here, trapped in shackles, rotting away.* (vv. 23-28).

Good news is coming, although Job only sees its faintest shadow. God does not leave us trapped and rotting. God is willing to dialogue and reason with us (Isaiah 1:18). Even more than that, God has made atonement for our sins through the sacrifice of Jesus Christ. The writer of Hebrews tells us to draw near to the throne of grace – God's throne – with boldness. Then we will find mercy and grace in our time of need. (Hebrews 4:16).

Meanwhile, Job is angry, frustrated, at God. We will see that his anger is misplaced. And yet anger draws Job toward God, not away from God. Incredibly, God is pleased by Job's boldness, and He does respond to Job's request. But for that, we will have to wait for chapter 38.

Job 14 (Waiting for Renewal)

Job continues his monologue: "Man who is born of a woman Is few of days and full of trouble." In other words, crap happens, and then you die. We are like the flowers that wither, the shadows that flee. But brevity does not mean levity. We know we are unclean, we know we are under judgment, and we chafe against our limitations. (vv. 1-4).

Job exclaims: *God, you did this! You determined our days, it is your gaze that burns. Look away for a while. Leave us alone, so perhaps we can find some small happiness.* (vv. 5-6).

Job imagines a hired worker resting under a tree, taking a break while the boss is busy elsewhere. *Wouldn't it be nice to be that hired worker. Wouldn't it be nice to be that tree!* "There is hope for a tree, if it be cut down, that it will sprout again." Stumps are notoriously difficult to remove. You think a stump is rotted, "yet at the scent of water it will bud and put out branches like a young plant." A tree holds the possibility of re-sprouting, renewing. (vv. 7-9). But what happens when a man is cut down, even in the prime of life? (v. 10).

We see our friends and family die, but we don't see any renewal. The river of life dries up, and that is the end. Or is it? "If a man dies, shall he live again?" (v. 10). What if the grave is only a temporary shelter? What if God could hide us there, until his anger has passed?

Job expresses his longing for the transcendent, for eternity: *Oh that you would appoint me a set time and remember me! I would wait patiently for my chance to re-sprout.* (vv. 13-14). "You would call, and I would answer you; you would long for the work of your hands." (v. 15). *Then, when you watched me, your eyes would sparkle with tenderness, not flash in anger. You would count my steps like a mother with her toddler.* (v. 16).

Something inside Job knows that he was made for a relationship with God. Something inside him knows he was made to respond to the call for resurrection. Job hopes against hope that God will call his name, just as Jesus called his friend Lazarus from the grave (John 11). God created Job, God must still have some affection for him.

But Job is also aware that he is unclean. A righteous man by human standards, Job cannot stand before the perfection of God. For Job to have a relationship with God, his sins must somehow be removed. *Oh that God would seal my transgression in a bag, and cover over my iniquity.* (v. 17). *But of course, that is impossible* (thinks Job.)

Even the mountains crumble away. Even boulders fall from their place. Just as water erodes the soil -- so you, God, destroy the hope of man! Instead of calling me, you send me away. I will pass, and you will prevail forever. (vv. 18-20). Job's current suffering has clouded his future hope. He turns inward, mourning the pain of his own body. *I will go to the grave without awareness. I will not see my future generations; their triumphs and successes will mean nothing to me.* (vv. 21-22).

Job barely glimpses the mystery of salvation. Yet what he seems dimly is not a mirage. In his spirit, Job will go on to join the great cloud of witnesses (Hebrews 12), as a model of steadfast endurance (James 5:11). In his spirit, Job will live to see Christ triumph over the grave. And some day – on The Day -- all believers, including Job, will hear the Savior's call to resurrection.

Interlude: The Gospel According to Job

Job was a righteous man who suffered great destruction. Specifically, God allowed Satan to take Job's wealth, his children, and his physical health. Over the course of the book of Job, we see Job and his friends engage in an extended dialogue, trying to process the painful thing that has happened.

Most of Job's speeches lament his personal and individual suffering. Chapter 14, which concludes the first cycle of speeches between Job and his three friends, is one example. Yet Job also touches – tentatively -- on important, broader principles. Inspired by the Holy Spirit, Job stumbles upon the gospel-in-embryo.

Unclean!

Job first remarks on mankind's basic problem: we are born of woman, few of days, and full of trouble. (14:1). We are mortal. Even more, our brief lives are not peaceful, but marred. Job asks, "And do you [God] open your eyes on such a one and bring me into judgment with you? Who can bring a clean thing out of an unclean? There is not one." (14:3-4).

Humanity is unclean and under God's judgment. Even though Job was uniquely righteous on earth (1:8), he knows he cannot escape his sinful nature as a human being. We are reminded of Romans 3:10: "None is righteous, no, not one." And again, the apostle Paul states, "Those who are in the flesh [i.e., born of woman] cannot please God." (Romans 8:8).

Job has described the existential predicament of mankind, and the origin of human suffering. We think of the first man-born-of-woman, Cain, whose offering was rejected, and who went on to murder his own brother (Genesis 4:1-16). The indelible imprint of Adam's fall has marked even the best of us.

Why can't God leave us alone?

Job proposes a solution, albeit not a very good one. He tells God: *since you made man like this - born of woman, few of days, and full of trouble - since you have set limits that man cannot pass - why don't you just leave us alone? Sure, human life is hard labor. But if you just stop scrutinizing us, perhaps we can find some enjoyment. You know, like a hired hand when the boss's back is turned.* (14:5-6).

At this point, Job and the gospel diverge. Becoming God's hired hand is just not an option. That was what the prodigal son suggested to his father in Christ's parable: "I have sinned, make me your hired hand." (Luke 15:18-19). Yet, sinful as we are, God does not allow us to exist as his paid workers.

God also refuses to leave us alone. No, he has greater plans than that. Man-born-of-woman is a slave to sin and corruption. But as believers, we are destined to become sons and daughters, even heirs of all God's world (Romans 8:17). As Paul says, "... you have received the Spirit of adoption as sons, by whom we cry, 'Abba! Father!'" (Romans 8:15). How does such an incredible transformation take place?

The Water of Renewal

Perhaps thinking about hired labor, Job imagines a tree that has been chopped down. That stump looks pretty pathetic, right? Yet, under the right conditions, "at the scent of water," the tree can sprout again. Stumps are surprisingly tenacious, and their roots can experience renewal (14:7-9).

But Job does not hold such hope for mankind. Instead of budding and putting out new branches, man shrivels up like a riverbed in the desert. As far as Job can tell, "man lies down and rises not again." (14:10-12). Job sees no "scent of water" to revive humanity.

Here again, Job is wrong. The gospel preaches just such a fountain of renewal. To the woman at the well, parched and used up, Jesus offered living water, water that becomes "a spring of water welling up to eternal life." (John 4:14). Jesus promises renewed life, even resurrection from the dead, for everyone who believes in him (John 11:25-26). But again, how exactly does this happen?

Tomb to Womb

Although Job did not have the full revelation of God, he saw the faint outlines of the gospel message. "Oh that you [God] would hide me in Sheol, that you would conceal me until your wrath be past, that you would appoint me a set time, and remember me!" (14:13). Job does not dispute that God's anger against mankind is justified. But if there is to be hope, somehow God has to hide us from God, until his wrath has passed over. Job imagines this could perhaps happen in Sheol, the grave.

Job sees Sheol both as an ending and a potential beginning. Job asks, "If a man dies, shall he live again?" (14:14). Can the tomb become a womb? In the Old Testament, the grave and the womb are often described in similar terms. For example, Psalm 139 speaks of David being "intricately woven in the depths of the earth," an expression that could refer to Sheol or his mother's body. Job makes use of this double meaning in chapter 3, where he curses the day of his birth and wishes the womb had become a tomb for him.

With his tomb-womb analogy, Job is onto something here. The only way for man to live again, the only way to experience renewal, is to die – with Christ. Believers are united with Christ in his death, and hidden with him in the grave (Romans 6:3-11; Colossians 3:3). The wrath of God has passed over us. Christ takes us from tomb to womb. As Jesus told Nicodemus, "... unless one is born of water and the Spirit, he cannot enter the kingdom of God." (John 3:5). We must be born again.

Call and Response

Job promises God, "All the days of my service I would wait, till my renewal should come." (14:13). This word "wait" can also be translated as "hope," or "trust." A baby in the womb doesn't have to do anything, except wait. Paul also talks about waiting eagerly, patiently, hopefully, for our renewal. (Romans 8:23-25).

How will Job know when it's time to come out? "You [God] would call, and I would answer you; you would long for the work of your hands." (14:15). Despite his great suffering, Job knows he belongs to God. He can't imagine God abandoning him. In fact, God longs for him. God will call, and Job will respond. As a mother is delivered from the pangs of childbirth, and rejoices in her baby, so Job's sorrow will be turned to joy when he sees God (John 16:21-22).

Anyone who believes in Christ has heard this call of God, and responded. Like Lazarus, we come forth from the grave. Even when we are most overwhelmed, "deep calls to deep." (Psalm 42:7) When God calls to our spirit, we can't help but answer (Romans 8:30). "The Spirit himself bears witness with our spirit that we are children of God." (Romans 8:16). This is the miracle of the new birth.

Sin Is Sealed

Once we hear God's call, and respond in faith, our relationship changes. God "numbers our steps," but not like a boss micro-managing us to make sure we hit our metrics. No, he watches like the father of a baby learning to walk. And God no longer sees our sin – that goes straight into the diaper genie. "My transgression would be sealed up in a bag, and you would cover over my iniquity." (14:17). God removes our sins "as far as the east is from the west" (Psalm 103:12).

As Paul puts it, "There is therefore now no condemnation for those who are in Christ Jesus. For the law of the Spirit of life has set you free in Christ Jesus from the law of sin and death." (Romans 8:1-2). The original problem raised by Job – can man be clean? can we come out from under God's judgment? – has been solved. We have been pruned clean, and God now dwells with us (John 14:3-4).

Must Suffering End in Despair?

Here, at the very point of salvation, Job's vision fails. Like a crumbling mountain or a flood that erodes the earth, suffering has shaken Job to his core. His hope is destroyed. "You [God] prevail against him [man], and he passes; you change his countenance, and send him away." (14:20). Again we are reminded of Cain, the first man-born-of-woman. When God ignored Cain's offering, Cain's countenance fell. You could see Cain's anger in his face, the anger that caused him to kill his brother Abel. And God sent Cain away.

Job's speech in chapter 14 ends on a low note. Job envisions man trapped in solitary suffering, cut off from future generations. How can we know whether our sons and daughters will succeed or fail? Is life limited to the lonely pain of our own bodies?

With the full revelation of the gospel, we know that suffering and decay are not signs that God has rejected us. We may very well experience tribulation, distress, persecution, famine, nakedness, danger or sword in this life (Romans 8:35). Yet we are more than conquerors through Christ, and nothing can separate us from God's love (Romans 8:37-39). Death is at work in our bodies, but our inner self is renewed day by day; our temporary suffering is preparing us for an eternal glory beyond compare (2 Corinthians 4:16-17).

What Job Did Not Yet Understand

At the very end of the book, God himself appears to Job. Faced with God's awesome power and majesty, Job recognizes the smallness of his thinking, of his very life (40:4-5). Job tells God, "I know that you can do all things, and that no purpose of yours can be thwarted... Therefore I have uttered what I did not understand, things too wonderful for me, which I did not know." (42:2-3).

Job recognizes God's sovereignty, and accepts it as good. God will accomplish his purposes. Job also seems to acknowledge the glimpses of the gospel given to him: wonderful things that he did not know, which he could not know at that time. In fact, Job's suffering as an innocent man foreshadowed the passion of Christ, our suffering savior.

Likewise, Job's restoration foreshadows our own. Job received back a double portion from the Lord, including sympathy, material blessing, and a new family with seven sons and three daughters. Before he died, Job saw his offspring to the fourth generation.

Sin, death, a saving birth, restoration: this is the gospel according to Job, now fully revealed in Christ. Peter tells us that the prophets "searched and inquired carefully," trying to discern the good news of the suffering and later glories of Christ. (1 Peter 1:10-12). These Old Testament saints, including Job, were serving us, looking forward to our time of revelation.

As New Testament Christians, we have God's clear word that our present suffering is not worth comparing with the glory that is to be revealed. (1 Peter 1:6-7). We have been given hope that "creation itself will be set free from its bondage to corruption and obtain the freedom of the glory of the children of God." (Romans 8:21). And we look forward, with the family of believers (including Job), to eternal joy in God's presence.

Job 15 (Life in the Desert)

Job's words shake his friends to the core. How can Job claim innocence, when God has clearly chosen him for disaster? How dare a mere man demand answers from God? Eliphaz erupts: *Your words are like hot air, blowing from desert haunts. Nothing good can come from such talk. You disrespect God, you hinder right worship. Who says such things? Sinners, that's who.* (vv. 1-6).

You think you are so wise. "Are you the first man who was born? Or were you brought forth before the hills?" (v. 7). *Are you a member of God's divine council? We know at least as much as you do, probably more. Some of us are older than your father!* (vv. 7-10).

But age is not the only measure of wisdom (Psalm 119:100). Our suffering transforms us, it changes our perspective, it complicates our worldview. When trouble hits us personally, we no longer see a simple cause-and-effect system. We skip the platitudes and hurl brash prayers to heaven. Our grief is raw, and this can make others uncomfortable.

Eliphaz continues: *We have been gentle with you. We have tried to comfort you with the words of God. Why are you still upset? Why do you keep saying offensive things? Remember you are only a man. God alone is perfect – even angels sin. And here you are, swimming in corruption. Why would God listen to you?* (vv. 11-16).

So far, Job has refused to be comforted. And Eliphaz, from his comfortable position, is offended. Eliphaz doesn't see Job's heart. Eliphaz doesn't understand how Job longs for God, reaches for God. Instead of responding in compassion, Eliphaz channels the accuser, Satan!

Let me tell you what I know, from wise and unbroken tradition. Wicked people are punished, period. The wicked man writhes in a lifetime of pain and despair. Sure, he may be prosperous for a while, but soon "dreadful sounds are in his ears" (v. 21) *and the destroyer comes upon him. He lives with a target on his back. He wanders far from home, begging for bread, terrified.* (vv. 17-24).

This is what happens to those who defy God. This is what happens to those who stubbornly fight God. (vv. 25-26). It's interesting that Eliphaz describes the rebellious man as one who "covered his face with his fat and gathered fat upon this waist." (v. 27). Perhaps this represents a life of self-indulgence. *Such people live in ruins, in poverty, in darkness.* (vv. 28-30).

Their lives are empty and unfruitful. Flames will dry up any shoots that look for renewal. If the wicked man is a vine, its grapes will drop off before they ripen. If the wicked man is an olive tree, it will cast off its blossoms before forming fruit. His life is barren and unfruitful - except for the poison fruit of evil plans. (vv. 31-35).

It is true that we often suffer the consequences of our sin. As James tells us, evil desire "when it has conceived gives birth to sin, and sin when it is fully grown gives birth to death." But we also know God can bring good fruit from dry and barren places. "The desert shall rejoice and blossom like the crocus... and rejoice with joy and singing." (Isaiah 35:1-2). Our present suffering, whether due to sin or not, is not the end.

But what do we do in the meantime? We don't have to choose between platitudes and despair. We can press on, continue to seek God. "Though the fig tree should not blossom, nor fruit be on the vines... yet I will rejoice in the Lord; I will take joy in the God of my salvation." (Habakkuk 3:17 - 18).

Job 16 (the Sufferer)

The debate has become personal; the gloves are off. Job responds: *Is this your idea of encouragement? You guys are miserable comforters, all of you. How can you keep repeating this stuff? 'God judges the wicked' – I know, I know! If you were in my shoes, I could say the exact same things to you. But I wouldn't do that.* (vv. 1-5).

In his suffering, Job longs for comforters whose mouths build up, whose words ease pain. Job imagines an alternate world where his friends are suffering instead. Job claims that, unlike his friends, he would know how to provide proper comfort.

So how do we comfort those who are suffering? The apostle Paul describes our God as the "God of all comfort, who comforts us in all our affliction..." He goes on to make the incredible statement, "For as we share abundantly in Christ's sufferings, so through Christ we share abundantly in comfort too." (2 Corinthians 3-7). When we suffer unjustly (as Job did), we share the sufferings of Christ. Through that process, we also share in the comfort of God the Father. And this experience enables us to walk alongside those who are suffering – without fear that we will somehow be "contaminated" -- and to share the overflow of divine comfort which we have received ourselves.

But Job has not yet experienced such comfort. *Whether I speak out or not, the pain just won't leave. God has worn me out, God has left me lonely, God has shriveled me up. You want to compare me to some stubborn fat guy (15:27)? Just look at me! My suffering has left me skin and bones.* (vv. 6-8).

At this point Job becomes macabre. *God – my enemy -- stalks me like a predatory animal, maliciously tearing me with sharp teeth.* (v. 9). Of course, God is not Job's enemy; the true prowling predator is Satan, to whom God gives limited power for a limited time. (1 Peter 5:8-10). Job continues: *Wicked men gape at me and strike me on the cheek, and God leaves me in their hands.* (vv. 10-11). We again glimpse parallels between Job's suffering and the sufferings of Christ, who was struck in the face on the way to crucifixion. (Psalm 22, Matt. 27:30).

God is the potter and I am the pot: He dashes me to pieces. God is the archer and I am the prey: He shoots me through the kidneys. God is the warrior and I am the city: He breaches my walls. Here I am groveling in the ashes, red-faced, with dark circles around my eyes, "although there is no violence in my hands, and my prayer is pure." (vv. 12-17).

Job doesn't realize it, but he is foreshadowing, even sharing in, Christ's sufferings. Isaiah 53 prophesies the coming of a suffering servant, "despised and rejected by men, a man of sorrows and acquainted with grief." This man would be pierced, crushed, "stricken, smitten by God, and afflicted." (Is. 53:3-5). All this would occur even though the servant was without deceit or violence (Is. 53:9). Most incredible of all, this suffering servant would bring us forgiveness, peace, and healing, so that we could experience God's comfort rather than his judgment (Is. 53:5).

Back in the moment, back in his pain, Job cries, "O earth, cover not my blood." (v. 18). Job imagines his blood crying out, like that of Abel, the first murder victim at the hands of Cain. (Genesis 4:10). Job wants justice, he doesn't want his suffering to pass without notice or meaning. Even though his friends scorn him, Job clings to the belief that he has an advocate in heaven. Job cries to this divine witness to plead his case with God. (v. 19). Job sees only fragments of the truth: Christ pleads our case, because Christ has suffered in our place. The blood of Christ speaks a better word than the blood of Abel (Hebrews 12:24).

The glimmer of hope is past, and Job once again turns to thoughts of death.

Interlude: Is God a Sadist?

Over the course of preparing these meditations, a somewhat irreverent question came up: Is God a sadist? God allowed Satan to torment Job, an innocent man, and destroy everything that Job held dear. Does this mean God is a cosmic bully? Does God take sick pleasure in evil?

Job's three friends - Eliphaz, Bildad and Zophar - don't want to touch this question with a 10-foot pole. Instead, they try to rearrange the facts to fit their worldview. God only brings suffering on evil people, they think. Therefore Job must have done something wrong, he must have a secret sin. But the truth is inescapable: Job is an innocent man. God deliberately chose an innocent person to suffer.

Job comes close to calling God a sadist. He says to God, "Does it seem good to you to oppress, to despise the work of your hands and favor the designs of the wicked?" (10:3). Job describes God as an enemy who "slashes open my kidneys and does not spare." (16:13). He oscillates between begging God to leave him alone (as if God were hopelessly cruel), and demanding a confrontation (as if Job could get God to see reason). And Job is a righteous man!

Let's take a step back here. To borrow a phrase from St. Paul, if God is a sadistic bully, "we are of all people most to be pitied." (I Corinthians 15:19). Of course, Christians don't believe that at all. We believe that God loves the world, that God is love (John 3:16, 1 John 4:8, 16). God takes no pleasure in the death of the wicked (Ezekiel 33:11), much less the suffering of his innocent servants.

So how do we reconcile God's love with the disaster that befell Job, or the relentless pains of our own lives? In the Christian narrative, innocent people sometimes suffer. In fact, the gospel hangs on the suffering of the one truly innocent person - the unblemished Lamb of God - Jesus. But our suffering is not meaningless. Our suffering is always for a higher purpose.

While sadists and abusive parents do exist on this earth, God is not like that. He is a good father. (Luke 11:13). And sometimes, even a good father must allow his children to suffer. If a child is sick, a good father will allow the temporary suffering of medical treatment: foul medicine or a painful operation. If a child is doing something harmful, a good father will use the temporary suffering of discipline: spanking or the loss of privileges. Job's fourth friend Elihu, in his rough way, elaborates some of these purposes (33:29-30).

To use another metaphor, a good military leader may have sincere affection, even love, for his troops. Yet that leader may still send his troops into danger, suffering, and even death for a higher purpose. There are noble reasons for suffering that make our pain worthwhile.

And there is a war going on. There _is_ a sadistic bully in the world, prowling like a lion, seeking souls to devour (1 Peter 5:8). It's our ancient foe, the devil. Satan orchestrated Job's suffering to extract maximum pain, and he enjoyed doing it. He is the thief that comes "only to steal and kill and destroy." (John 10:10). The very reason the Son of God appeared, and suffered, and died, was to destroy the works of the devil (1 John 3:8). And often, that dark hour where Satan roars in sadistic pride, is the moment of our salvation.

This is the essence of faith – to believe that "this light momentary affliction is preparing for us an eternal weight of glory beyond all comparison." (I Corinthians 4:17). Like Job, we don't get all the answers, at least not in the moment. But also like Job, we have the hope of seeing God – who reveals himself in chapter 38.

Job 17 (Not Alone)

Job again wallows in his misery. *My spirit is broken, my life is over. I can see the Grim Reaper standing by. And next to him, my so-called friends. Even when I close my eyes, I see their mocking faces.* (vv.1-2).

God, won't you vouch for me? No one else is coming to bail me out. In chapter 16, Job describes in graphic detail how God has crushed him. And yet, we see Job returning to God for help. *God, you have blinded my so-called friends to the truth. You can't let them win! If someone betrays his friends, may his children be cursed!* (vv. 3-5).

After that brief interlude, Job returns to his favorite topic, his suffering. *People talk behind my back, spit in front of my face. My eyes have burned themselves out, my body is just a shadow.* (vv. 6-7). But then, we read a strange, almost hopeful turn in Job's monologue. The mockers are not the only ones watching. *The righteous see me and are appalled. They are angry with the godless, they hold to the right, and their clean hands grow stronger.* (vv. 8-9).

Incredibly, Job has enough presence of mind to admit he is not the only righteous person on earth. Although he is surrounded by false friends who have betrayed him, Job recognizes that there is always a righteous remnant. Perhaps Job's perseverance in suffering will be a testimony to these witnesses. Job trusts that these godly people will also hold to what is right, and that they will grow stronger -- even as he is growing weaker.

When we suffer, it is easy to think we are alone. At one point, the prophet Elijah was running for his life from Queen Jezebel. Alone in the wilderness, Elijah told God he might as well die. God was kind enough to meet with Elijah, and to reveal that Elijah was not alone: he was one of seven thousand Israelites that had not turned away to idols (1 Kings 19). We also know that there were "secret agents" even in Jezebel's own household -- for example,

Obadiah, who hid a hundred of God's prophets in a cave and smuggled food to them (1 Kings 18).

Back in Job chapter 17, when the righteous remnant see Job, they are horrified. They mourn and are angry along with Job. If only Job could see just a little bit farther. If only Job could believe that one day, the godly would see him and rejoice, not mourn (Psalm 119:74).

Job returns to his pain and his detractors. *I'm looking for a wise man, but I won't find him with any of you. It's over for me, only broken plans and frustrated desires. You can't turn night into day. How can you say light is near, when all I see is darkness? My hope is dead and buried. The dark pit is my father, the worms are my mother and sister.* (vv. 10-14).

I think about the childhood taunt "Nobody loves me, everybody hates me, guess I'll go eat worms." In a healthy emotional state, we find worms disgusting – pale, slimy, feeding on decay. But in a depressed state, we feel strange emotional connections to these pathetic creatures.

"Where then is my hope?" asks Job, "Who will see my hope? Will it go down to the bars of the grave? Shall we [me and my hope] descend together into the dust?" (vv. 15-16). Job's cry is heartbreaking.

And yet... we do have a Hope that descended into the grave, on our behalf. Our Hope not only descended, but also ascended in resurrected glory. And so we look forward to our own resurrection, where death will be swallowed up in victory. The Grim Reaper will not have the final word.

Job 18 (Horror Story)

Job has spent the past two chapters wallowing in despair and complaining about his "miserable comforters." This offends Bildad. Why does Job continue to ignore the counsel of his friends, continue to dispute conventional wisdom? Why hasn't Job admitted the obvious -- his troubles must be punishment for his sin!

Bildad erupts: *How long will you keep looking for words to justify yourself? You think we are stupid, even bovine.* (vv. 2-3). "Shall the earth be forsaken for you, or the rock be removed out of its place?" (v. 4). Job is challenging the foundations of Bildad's world view. For a righteous man to suffer, that would change the order of the universe! Bildad doubles down on his diatribe.

The light of the wicked man flickers out. He schemes, and is snared in his own trap. (vv. 5-10). In other words, Job, your pain is your own damn fault. This sounds a lot like the book of Proverbs, which tells us that "The light of the righteous rejoices, but the lamp of the wicked will be put out." (Proverbs 13:9). And also, "Whoever digs a pit will fall into it, and a stone will come back on him who starts it rolling." (Proverbs 26:27). So God absolutely promises to bring justice and punish all wicked oppressors.

But this does not mean that anyone walking in darkness, anyone in trouble or trapped, is under God's curse. In fact, the suffering servant of Isaiah - appointed by God to bring justice - sees our suffering and brings hope, not condemnation. According to the prophecy, "a bruised reed he will not break, and a faintly burning wick he will not quench." (Isaiah 42:3). Christ came to be "a light for the nations, to open the eyes that are blind, to bring out the prisoners from the dungeon, from the prison those who sit in darkness." (Isaiah 42:6-7). God loves both justice and mercy.

What a contrast to the characters we meet in Bildad's cautionary tale, now become horror story. *Terror chases the wicked man, his strength is wasted, he stumbles while Calamity eagerly watches.* (vv.

11-12). Even worse, out of the darkness emerges the Firstborn of Death, a devouring monster that tears at skin and limbs. As if that wasn't enough, his carcass is dragged before The King of Terrors. Thus the wicked man perishes. (vv. 13-14). Meanwhile, to complete the tale, his home is vandalized and burned to the ground. The wicked man has no name or posterity left behind... nothing but a creepy tale to tell around the campfire. (vv. 15-20).

Bildad ends with the moral of the story: "Surely such are the dwellings of the unrighteous, such is the place of him who knows not God." (v. 21). This is no encouragement to Job, as we will see in the next chapter.

But we can be encouraged, because we have the rest of the story. The Firstborn of Death will not have the last word. There will be a great reversal; the consumer will himself be consumed. Isaiah promises that the Lord "will swallow up death forever." (Isaiah 25:8). Death will be "swallowed up in victory." (2 Corinthians 15:54). We may suffer as innocent victims, or suffer due to our own bad choices. (Most likely, both). We can put our anger aside, because God is our vengeance. We can put our shame aside, because God is our redeemer.

May we allow our suffering to show us our need for God. And may we look to Jesus, the suffering servant, for our salvation.

Job 19 (He Lives)

And now we come to chapter 19, where Job declares, "I know that my Redeemer lives!" This is the passage that has inspired generations of beautiful music, from George F. Handel to Nicole C. Mullin. However, there are 24 verses between us and this blessed confession. And I can't imagine these verses being sung by a choir.

First, Job lashes out at his friends: "How long will you torment me and break me in pieces with words?" *Let's assume, for the sake of argument, that I have done wrong. What does that have to do with you? Are you shaming me to make yourself look better?* (vv.1-5). Sticks and stones may break our bones... and words may break our spirits. Yes, Job's companions are miserable comforters.

Then Job launches into all the ways God has done him wrong. *God has trapped me in his net, bricked up my way, dropped darkness on my road. God has stripped my glory, broken me down, uprooted my hope. God has burned against me like an enemy, and his armies have besieged me.* (vv. 6-12).

That doesn't sound like God! What about the God who forgives, who heals, who redeems? What about the God "who crowns you with steadfast love and mercy," and "who satisfies you with good so that your youth is renewed like the eagle's"? (Psalm 103). This incongruity is part of Job's lament. In his prior life, Job knew God's goodness and favor. Job thought he was God's friend, and yet now God is treating him like an enemy. Where has Job's God gone?

"Behold, I cry out 'Violence!' but I am not answered; I call for help, but there is no justice." (v. 7). Not only does God not rescue Job, there is no one to rescue him from God.

The people around Job only contribute to his suffering. He describes his pitiful situation: *My family has failed me, my friends have forgotten me. My guests treat me like I am the foreigner; my servants refuse to speak to me. My wife won't kiss me (she says I*

*have bad breath) and my brothers won't hug me (they say I have
B.O.) Little kids despise me, and even my dearest loved ones hate
me and betray me. I am skin and bones, there is nothing left of me.*
(vv. 13-20).

"Have mercy on me, have mercy on me, O you my friends, for
the hand of God has touched me!" (v. 21). But Job's friends do not
rescue him either; like God – or so it appears to Job – they pursue
and attack him. (v. 22).

In the midst of this overwhelming pain, abandoned by God and
his loved ones, Job suddenly cries out – *Somebody get a pen and
write this down! You are going to want to remember this!* (v. 23-24):

"For I know that my Redeemer lives, and at the last he will stand
upon the earth. And after my skin has been thus destroyed, yet in
my flesh I shall see God, whom I shall see for myself, and my eyes
shall behold, and not another. My heart faints [with longing] within
me!" (vv. 25-27).

Despite everything, Job declares that his relationship with God
will be restored. In fact, his body will also be restored, and he will
see God with his own eyes. This will happen because Job has an
Advocate, a Redeemer, who will come to earth and intercede on his
behalf. We believe this Redeemer has come, that He has overcome
sin and death, and that He will come again. We believe that, with
Job, we will be resurrected and see God with our own eyes, because
of the work of our Redeemer. (1 John 3:2).

Emboldened, Job turns again to his companions. *If you keep
blaming me and coming after me, be warned! There is a judgment
for false accusers.* (vv. 28-29).

Job 20 (Belly Ache)

In chapter 19, Job throws himself on the mercy of his Redeemer – and also tells his friends they better stop the false accusations. This does not sit well with Zophar. In his first speech, Zophar tried to end on a positive note: repent from sin, turn to God and all will be well! (ch. 11:13-19). But this time, Zophar goes for the fire and brimstone.

I'm insulted, says Zophar, but you can't change my mind. This has been the way of the world since the beginning. Sure, the wicked experience happiness -- for a moment. Don't be fooled when evil people rise to the heavens, head in the clouds. They will get flushed like a turd. "Uhhh... where did he go?" The wicked man flies away like a dream. Now you see him, now you don't. He will be forced to give back his ill-gotten gain, while his kids go begging. Despite his healthy appearance, he will die an untimely death. (vv. 1-11).

Zophar then begins an extended discourse on the paradox of greed. *The wicked follow their desires endlessly, but without satisfaction. In fact, what they consume ends up consuming them. Evil tastes sweet in the mouth, so sweet that people don't want to let it go. Yet it turns to poison in their stomach.* (vv. 12-14). Grotesquely, the evil man "swallows down riches and vomits them up again; God casts them out of his belly." (v. 15).

Zophar continues: *The wicked man will not see true flourishing, will not see the promised land flowing with milk and honey. The wicked man cannot keep the fruit of his toil, cannot enjoy the profit of his trading. This is what happens to those who obtain riches by oppressing the poor.* (vv. 16-19).

We know from many different Bible passages that God defends the cause of the oppressed (Psalm 72:12-14; Proverbs 22:22-23; Isaiah 10:1-3; etc.). We also see a direct contrast between God's promises to the wicked, and His promises to the righteous man, firmly planted by streams of water, fruitful and prosperous (Psalm

1); or to the righteous woman, whose trading is profitable, who cares for the poor, and who laughs at the future (Proverbs 31). So we know there is some truth in Zophar's words. Unfortunately, his words are wrongly applied to Job, who is described as a righteous man (Job 1:1).

Zophar continues to describe the distress, gastric and otherwise, of the wicked man. *He knows no contentment in his belly* (v. 20). *He consumes until there is nothing left* (v.21). *But his over-fullness will lead to distress; those he persecuted will turn against him. God will fill his belly with burning hail!* (v. 23). *Terror, violence, darkness, fire: his treasure will be trapped, and he himself will be devoured. In the day of God's wrath, heaven and earth will rise against the wicked man (did I already mention his possessions would be carried away?) And this is the decree of the Lord.* (vv. 24-29).

Again, Zophar communicates some truths. The apostle Paul speaks of God's enemies in a similar manner, including the reference to bellies: "Their end is destruction, their god is their belly, and they glory in their shame, with minds set on earthly things." (Philippians 3:19). But we, like Job, have faith in our Redeemer from heaven (Hebrews 10:39).

This is the last time we hear from Zophar. Eliphaz and Bildad each have three speeches, but Zophar only speaks twice. Some Bible scholars speculate that a portion of the book of Job was lost. At any rate, God in His wisdom did not preserve for us any further words from Zophar.

Job 21 (The Rich and Famous)

In the last chapter, Zophar described the destruction of the evil man in salacious, almost gloating detail. The judgment of the Lord will fall on the wicked!

Job answers: *It's my turn to "comfort" you. And when I'm done, you can mock on. You don't need to tell gruesome stories, I am a walking horror show. I creep myself out. And the truly terrifying part is when people tell me that this is the judgment of the Lord.* (vv. 1-6).

Hello -- have you seen an actual wicked person lately? Lifestyles of the rich and famous! They have great kids, they live in gated communities, no "rod of God" is upon them. Their investments continue to grow [which they don't hesitate to point out]. They sing and dance and play with their grandkids. And when their time comes, they pass peacefully in their sleep. All the while they blatantly ignore the God who showers them with blessing. "Why should we serve God? What profit is there in prayer?" I reject their counsel. But how often, really, is the lamp of the wicked put out? (vv. 7-17).

Job wants to believe in the righteous judgment of God, but he just doesn't see it. Believers through the ages have struggled with the same question (see, Psalm 73). God's children suffer, while dictators rampage and celebrities flaunt their excess on Instagram. We cry out with the psalmist, "O my God, make [your enemies] like whirling dust, like chaff before the wind. As fire consumes the forest, as the flame sets the mountains ablaze, so may you pursue them with your tempest and terrify them with your hurricane!" (Psalm 83:13-14)

But Job asks: *how often does this really happen? (v. 18). Don't try to explain God, saying, maybe God is saving up their punishment for their children. Let God's wrath fall on them personally, that they might know it! Why do they care what happens after they are gone?* (vv. 19-21).

All this is above my pay grade, of course, but it seems so arbitrary. One person lives and dies in ease, with his "udders full" and his "marrow moist." Another person lives in poverty and dies in bitterness. Then both return to dust and become worm food. Is there any meaning in this world? (vv. 22-26).

Job's friends have provided pat answers and simplistic explanations. "Good people are blessed by God. Thus, your suffering must be punishment for sin in your life." But Job looks around him, and sees wicked people having a great time. Then Job looks at his own life and doesn't understand what he has done to deserve total destruction. The words of Job's friends do not match his experience.

Job continues: *If you don't believe me, ask those who have traveled abroad. They will tell you the same thing: disaster steps around the evil man. No one stands up to him, no one criticizes him to his face, no one repays him for what he has done. When he dies, he gets a fancy memorial and his funeral procession ties up traffic for miles. "All mankind follows after him, and those who go before him are innumerable." (v. 33). Tell me, why should I be comforted by your falsehoods and empty nothings?* (v. 34).

Jon Bloom writes, "Prolonged exposure to confounding darkness is a wearisome experience (Psalm 73:16)... We probably thought ourselves more a match for it in the optimistic bloom of youth, but experience put us in our place. The evil is beyond our strength and our comprehension. Hope can take a beating... until we remember." We must remember God's promise, that night will end and we will see the face of Christ.

Job 22 (No Charity)

Job stubbornly insists that prosperity doesn't automatically follow obedience. An angry Eliphaz begins his third and final speech: *God doesn't need your help Job. Help yourself instead. Quit insisting that you are right.* "Is it any pleasure to the Almighty if you are in the right, or is it gain to him if you make your ways blameless?" (v. 3).

For the record, the opening story tells us that God is, in fact, pleased with Job. God brags on Job to Satan, twice! (Job 1:8, 2:3). There is a sense in which God places His own reputation on the line by allowing Satan to test Job. Eliphaz seems to be repeating the message from the night spirit: God views humans as nothing (Job 4:17-21). But this spirit lied about God's view of man, and especially about his view of Job.

Eliphaz continues: *So what's the alternative -- you want me to believe that God is judging you <u>because</u> you fear and honor him? That doesn't make any sense! Just admit that you are wrong.* "Is not your evil abundant? There is no end to your iniquities." (v. 5). Eliphaz launches into a litany of accusations against Job: *You extorted your brothers. You stripped the naked. You denied water and food to the needy. You showed favoritism to the powerful. You turned away widows and crushed the strength of the fatherless. How do I know this? Because you are being punished by traps and terrors and darkness and flood. There is no other explanation.* (vv. 6-11).

Of course, charity has always been an important component of the Christian faith. The law of Moses required the Israelites to treat strangers, widows and orphans fairly (Exodus 22:21-24). Similarly, in the New Testament, James says, "Religion that is pure and undefiled before God the Father is this: to visit orphans and widows in their affliction, and to keep oneself unstained from the world." (James 1:27). Jesus closely identifies with those who are suffering from hunger, thirst, loneliness, nakedness, sickness and imprisonment. In one sobering passage, Jesus states that our very salvation will be judged based on how we treated "the least of these" (Mathew 25:31-46).

Eliphaz is claiming that Job lacks these markers of a follower of God. However, we know that Job is righteous. We also learn later, in chapter 29, that Job did care for the poor and needy (29:12-17). Eliphaz bases his false accusations solely upon the suffering that Job is experiencing. But wouldn't that mean that Job is now one of "the least of these," and deserving of compassion himself?

Eliphaz goes on to accuse Job of hiding secret sin. *Look at the night sky, see how high God is. But you think God can't see you from that distance. You are ignoring the destruction of the wicked who have walked that way before you.* Eliphaz takes Job's description of the wicked in chapter 21:14-16 and spits it back at Job. *Wicked men said to God, "Depart from us," and "What can the Almighty do to us?" All the while they blatantly ignored the God who showers them with blessing. I reject their counsel. Why shouldn't the righteous be glad and mock the wicked when they are cut off?*

Then Eliphaz changes tactics, issuing a heart-felt call to repentance. *Submit to God and be at peace! Good will come to you if you receive instruction from the Lord. Return to the Lord and be built up. Lay your gold in the dust, and the Almighty will be your treasure. Delight yourself in the Lord, and he will hear you. Your decisions will be established, and light will shine on your ways. If you will only humble yourself, he will lift you up. And you in turn can be an agent of salvation to other sinners.*

These are wonderful promises, echoing many similar Scripture passages. But in this case, they are wrongly applied to Job.

Job 23 (Seat of God)

Job has been wrongly accused of oppressing the poor and violating God's law. Slander has been piled on top of all Job's other suffering. "Today also my complaint is bitter; my hand is heavy on account of my groaning" (v. 1). Where can Job go for justice?

Job longs to enter God's heavenly courtroom, but he doesn't know where to find it. Job imagines explaining the whole situation to God, and finally hearing God's answer. Job recognizes God's great power, including the ability to win every debate! Nonetheless Job imagines God voluntarily handicapping Himself, putting everything else aside to listen to Job's argument. (vv. 3-6). Under these conditions – where God Himself has leveled the playing field – Job imagines being "acquitted forever." (v.7).

Thankfully, the way to acquittal in God's courtroom has been revealed. As Job imagined, God did handicap himself, taking the humble form of a man doomed to die (Philippians 2:6-8). And by his death, Jesus became the Way to the Father (John 14:6). For this reason, we can approach the seat of God with confidence, receiving His grace and mercy (Hebrews 4:16), just as Job imagined.

But for Old Testament saints like Job, these mysteries were hidden. Peter tells us that the prophets (and I would include Job here) "searched and inquired carefully, inquiring what person or time the Spirit of Christ in them was indicating when he predicted the sufferings of Christ and the subsequent glories." And in this diligent searching, Job was serving not himself, but us, the future saints. (1 Peter 1:10-12). What a long and difficult search it was!

Job says: "Behold, I go forward, but he is not there, and backward, but I do not perceive him; on the left hand when he is working, I do not behold him; he turns to the right hand, but I do not see him." (v. 8-9). *But even though I do not see God, God sees me! And I will be refined by this trial!* Peter agrees: through suffering, our faith will be tested and found more precious than gold (1 Peter 1:6-7). Though we do not see God now, we believe (I Peter 1:8).

I believe! says Job. *I have walked faithfully in God's ways. I treasure the words from God's mouth more than my daily bread* (v. 12). These are the words of a man after God's own heart. These are the words of Christ himself, tested by Satan in the desert: "Man shall not live by bread alone, but by every word that comes from the mouth of God." (Matthew 4:4).

And then the curtain falls once more. *God doesn't change, he does what he wants to do.* "For he will complete what he appoints for me" (v. 14) *and so far, it looks like all horrible things. How could I have imagined being in God's presence? He terrifies me, he has made my heart faint. You were right about one thing, Eliphaz: thick darkness covers my face and I cannot see* (v. 17; compare 22:10-11).

Job rejects the "God-in-a-box" described by his friends. Job knows God will not be manipulated, does not operate by formula. But how *does* God operate then? Job fears that God's sovereignty will lead to yet more pain. Perhaps you have had this fear as well – God can do anything he wants – which means, God can do things I don't want.

But we have promises: "For those who love God all things work together for good" (Romans 8:28) and "he who began a good work in you will bring it to completion at the day of Jesus Christ" (Philippians 1:6). God will complete what he has appointed for Job, and for us. And though the way is paved with suffering – after all, Christ, the Way, was the suffering servant – the end will be good and glorious.

Job 24 (The Widow's Ox)

Job abruptly looks away from his own suffering, and pleads on behalf of all the oppressed. *God, why haven't you come in judgment? Injustice is endless.* Job calls attention to the immoral acts around him: *thieves move ancient boundary lines and steal entire flocks; lenders cruelly repossess the orphan's donkey and the widow's ox; brutes run the poor off the road.* (vv. 1-4). Skipping ahead to verse 9, perhaps most traumatic: *Babies are snatched from their mothers, taken as a pledge against the poor.*

Today, these crimes sound anachronistic – when was the last time you saw a widow with an ox? Yet modern equivalents are not hard to find. Corporate greed that promotes mindless borrowing and shakes the stock market. Phone and internet scammers who prey on the elderly and confused. Policies that incentivize the breakdown of the family, creating a cycle of struggling single mothers. Companies, both legal and illegal, that encourage women to sell or abort their babies as a solution to poverty.

And what can those poor people do? They scatter and hide; they labor and seek food for their children in the wasteland. They glean animal fodder and eat what the wicked have cast away. They shiver without adequate clothing; they are rain-drenched, homeless; they are left clinging to a rock. With growling stomachs, the hungry harvest grain for others; their throats are parched as they tread the winepress. (vv. 5-11).

Job describes the pitiful condition of the poor around him. I wonder, did his suffering make him more sensitive to the suffering of others? We know Job was a kind man before his trials (see chapter 29). But perhaps this close kinship with the poor was something new. When we suffer, we learn to mourn with those who mourn (Romans 12:15). We are able to comfort with the comfort we have received (2 Corinthians 1:3-7). After my son was diagnosed with a brain disorder, I gained instant empathy for parents going through similar hardships. And even a "small" tribulation -- like potty-training your child - is hard to share with friends who have never walked that road.

But Job has found no comfort for his sorrow, at least not yet. "From out of the city the dying groan, and the soul of the wounded cries for help; yet God charges no one with wrong." (v. 12). *Is there no justice?*

The darkness of Job's suffering (23:17) finds a mirror in the moral darkness around him. "There are those who rebel against the light," (v. 13) who do not walk the path of God's word (Psalm 119:105). *Murderers, thieves, adulterers - they wait for darkness so they can do their evil deeds in secret. Like vampires, they shut themselves up during the day. The same darkness that terrorizes me is a friend to the wicked.* (v. 17). Light clarifies and exposes. People who do wicked things hate the light and remain in darkness. (John 3:19-21).

Verse 18 has caused some trouble for translators, but it appears that Job is calling a curse on evil oppressors: *May they be washed away, may their vineyards be barren. Just as the drought snatches away the snow melt, may the grave snatch away the wicked. From womb to worm, may they be forgotten and their wickedness broken.* Job hates those who hate God (Psalm 119:21-22). Even though Job is suffering, even though his friends accuse him of wickedness, Job still clings to right and wrong.

Job continues: *Even while they mistreat widows, the wicked enjoy power, good health, financial security. But this is only temporary. They will be brought low. Mark my words, the Grim Reaper will come for the wicked.* (vv. 21-25). With unusual clarity, Job reassures us - and himself -- that God will judge in his own time.

Job 25-26 (The Fleeing Serpent)

A celebrity rises to prominence, perhaps even political office. Suddenly, we are told that this individual is racist! or sexist! based on an alleged incident from years ago. The mob rushes to social media, demanding justice from its chosen victim: apologize, step down, submit to the ruin you deserve.

What if the victim refuses to apologize, and demands justice for himself instead? Imagine the rage of the mob. Now imagine the rage of Job's three friends, as Job stubbornly clings to his own innocence.

We have navigated two full cycles of dialogue between Job and his friends – Eliphaz, Job, Bildad, Job, Zophar, Job; Eliphaz II, Job, Bildad II, Job, Zophar II, Job. But in this third round -- Eliphaz III, Job, Bildad III -- the dialogues come to an abrupt stop. In a 6-verse finale, Bildad rails at Job: *Fear the rule of the Lord! Behold the stars, his countless heavenly armies. Yet God shines still brighter. Man is a maggot, a worm in God's eyes. How dare you claim that you are righteous?* (25:1-6).

Job retorts, sarcastically: *Thank you for helping the helpless! Thank you for saving the weak, for counseling the stupid! Thank you, oh thank you!* (26:1-4).

Fear God? Yeah I fear God! The underworld trembles, even Death and Destruction lie naked before Him. God who stretches out the heavens, hangs the world in space; God who bags the rain in thunderclouds, covers the moon in shadow; God who draws the horizon. A rebuke from God shakes the pillars of heaven. (vv. 5-11). "By his power he stilled the sea." (v. 12) *His wisdom shattered the Chaos Monster, his breath blew darkness from the heavens.* "His hand pierced the fleeing serpent." (v. 13).

In the act of creation, God tamed the primordial sea of chaos (Genesis 1:2). He even made the sea fruitful, teeming with marine life (Genesis 1:20). Later, God saved the Hebrews by dividing the waters of the Red Sea, allowing them to pass on dry land – and then closing the sea over the armies of Pharaoh (Exodus 14:21 – 29). Much later, Jesus demonstrated the power of God by rebuking the wind and the waves, creating instant calm on the Sea of Galilee (Luke 8:24). The disciples marveled: "Who then is this, that he commands even winds and water, and they obey him?" (Luke 8:25). Only God can do that!

But who is the fleeing serpent? We are reminded of another passage, from Isaiah: "In that day the Lord with his hard and great and strong sword will punish Leviathan the fleeing serpent, Leviathan the twisting serpent, and he will slay the dragon that is in the sea." (Isaiah 27:1). Since the Garden of Eden, the serpent or dragon has been associated with Satan (Genesis 3:1). In addition to the destructive forces of nature, there are darker, spiritual forces working in the world as well. Just as Christ tamed the sea, he will come to pierce the serpent forever (Revelation 20).

Not satisfied with the Red Sea miracle, Moses asked to see God's glory. God agreed, with certain limits for Moses' own protection. God would hide Moses in a rocky crevice, and then after God had already passed, Moses would be able to see God's back. (Exodus 33:22-23). That was all Moses could handle.

Job concludes: *Everything we know is but the smallest whisper, the fringe of his garment. Truly, the power of God is beyond understanding.* (v. 14). Yet, in Christ, God gave us more than a whisper, more than his back as he passed us by: he gave us himself. Christ suffered for us, he endured the rage of the mob for us. He is with us in our suffering now, and he will end all suffering forever. Bildad was wrong, we are not worms and maggots to God. In the fringe of Christ's garment, the outcast found healing and forgiveness (Luke 8:44). And so can we.

Job 27 (Test Passed?)

Now that Job's friends are done speaking, Job issues a final, bold rebuke. *God has denied my claim and made my soul bitter. Nonetheless, God lives – and his Spirit lives in me. As long as I draw breath from that Spirit, I will not speak lies. I will not concede that you, my friends, are right. I will not deny my integrity. I cling to my righteousness with no regrets.* (vv. 1-6).

This is an amazing passage. Job sees clearly that God has intentionally allowed suffering in his life. Job continues to feel pain, and he continues to believe that justice has been denied to him. Yet Job does not deny God. Instead, he proclaims that God lives! More than that, Job declares that God's Spirit continues to dwell with him! When his trials first began, Job longed for death (ch. 3). Yet here he is, some 24 chapters later, still suffering, but still alive.

As long as God continues to give him life, Job boldly refuses the platitudes of his accusers. Instead, Job commits to speak the truth as best he understands it. "I hold fast my righteousness and will not let it go." (v. 6). What does this mean, to "hold fast my righteousness"?

As New Testament Christians, we sometimes have a hard time understanding the "righteousness" of Old Testament saints. Doesn't Paul say "all have sinned"? (Romans 3:23). Isn't our salvation based on grace alone, through faith alone? (Ephesians 2:8-9). Yes, and that is just the beginning. Old Testament righteousness also came through faith. Abraham the patriarch "believed the Lord, and he counted it to him as righteousness." (Genesis 15:6). Hebrews 11 chronicles the faith of more than a dozen Old Testament heroes. But – for both Old and New Testament followers of God – we must demonstrate our faith by obedience (John 14:15; James 2:18).

Job is obedient to what he knows about God. The Lord calls Job "my servant," "a blameless and upright man, who fears God and turns away from evil." (Job 1:8). God praises Job for holding fast to his integrity in the midst of terrible loss (Job 2:3). Satan does his best to turn Job's loyalty away from God; so does Job's wife (Job 2:9). Job's so-called friends misuse theological principles and try to browbeat Job into a false confession. Yet Job remains committed to God and committed to the truth, demonstrating his steadfast faith (James 5:11).

Next Job takes the theology of his tormentor-friends, and turns it back on them. *You have chronicled the curses of the wicked, meaning them for me – may those same curses fall on my enemies. When the godless are cut off, what hope do they have? Will an evil man call upon God, and will God hear his cry? It's my turn to teach you about the hand of God. We all observe the same things, so why are you talking empty nonsense?* (vv. 7-12).

The wicked man will inherit disaster. Sword, famine and pestilence plague his family. He may accumulate wealth – piles of silver and clothing – but it will be given to the righteous. He builds a cocoon like a moth, but undergoes a reverse metamorphosis: he goes to sleep rich and wakes up poor. A flood of terror, a whirlwind of nightmares! The wicked man flees even as he is swept away. The ghosts of the desert hiss at his heels. (vv. 13-23).

At this point in the story, Job has not yet seen God's deliverance. And yet, it seems that his crisis of faith has passed. Satan predicted that Job would curse God to his face (1:11, 2:8). For sure, Job has been discouraged and angry, yet he has not forsaken God. Job declares that he will cling to the path of obedience the rest of his life, short or long, whatever that life might hold. He has passed the test.

Job 28:1-11 (Gold Rush)

My husband is a big fan of the reality show "Gold Rush," set in the Alaskan wilderness. Tough men – and a few brave women – go to extreme lengths to extract gold flecks from the ground. At the end of a bone-jarring, ear-splitting week of running heavy equipment, the crew crowds around the scales. How many ounces did they recover this time? Will they make their season goal?

God in his wisdom placed valuable minerals deep within the earth. Since the beginning of history, men have given up comforts and risked their lives to search for this treasure. In chapter 28, Job begins an extended meditation on this fascinating human activity.

"Surely there is a mine for silver," says Job, "and a place for gold that they refine." *Men take iron out of the earth, use white hot fires to smelt impurities from copper ore. To reach these precious materials, the treasure-hunters travel far beneath the earth's surface, in deep darkness, in the "shadow of death." These men put an end to darkness, bringing their light with them as they search out deep caverns (v. 3).*

Job has often described his suffering in terms of darkness and gloom (ex. Job 3:4-5, 10:21-22, 23:16-17). Yet here we see a different side to darkness – it can be penetrated by light, it can be searched out, it can be forced to give up priceless treasure. But there is a cost.

The miner digs his shaft far away from human habitation, in a wilderness forgotten by travelers. He hangs in the air, he swings precariously. Farmers plant the surface of the earth to bring forth bread, but they don't know what is underneath. Turn over the earth, and in the burnt remains you will find stones of sapphire, dust of gold. (vv. 4-6).

God knows we must work for our daily bread, and he promises to provide it. But Job seems to urge us, dig deeper. Look for the treasure. Jesus also told parables of treasure. The kingdom of heaven is like a man who found treasure buried in a field, and then sold everything to buy the field (Matthew 13:44). Precious metals and stones, deeply buried, provide glimpses of our heavenly home, with jeweled gates and golden streets (Revelation 21:21). When we think about treasure-hunters, we have to ask, what is worth risking our comforts for? Is earthly treasure a metaphor for something greater and more beautiful?

Job continues: *Although the hawk flies high, its keen eye does not see the path to the treasure mine. Nor does the proud lion tread that road.* (vv. 7-8). I think this couplet has a double meaning. The mining operation is remote (v. 4), but it also requires innocence and humility, not predation and aggression. Job is describing something more profound than a Gold Rush.

Man rips mountains by the roots, cuts out channels, sees every precious thing (v. 9-10). *He dams up streams and brings what is hidden to light* (v.11). That is some serious earth-scaping.

And I wonder, are we still talking about mining, or are we talking about miracles? Isaiah promised that someday the mountains would move, and the glory of the Lord, previously hidden, would be revealed. (Isaiah 40:3-5). Does Job glimpse Christ in the man who puts an end to darkness, who searches out to the farthest limit? For even in the darkness, even in the wilderness, we are God's treasure (1 Peter 2:4) and He is ours (Psalm 16:5-6).

The path to treasure is treacherous. Perhaps Job's suffering is part of that path. Perhaps we must experience the darkness for our eyes to be truly opened.

Interlude: Metaphorphosis

As we have seen, Job 28 is a vivid, extended metaphor on the rigors of mining: living far from civilization, digging in darkness, swinging pick-axe to rock. Yet the rewards outweigh the risk. Job's miner uncovers sapphires, gold, treasure. In the second half of the chapter, Job draws an analogy to the search for wisdom.

Job's description is so detailed, it is worthy of extended meditation. And I wonder, how did these precious metals and stones, shining in soft glow or hard brilliance, come to hide under the surface of the earth? Why are they so desirable, yet so difficult to obtain? As a Christian, I believe God put them there, and I believe He put them there for a purpose. But was part of that purpose to act as a metaphor, to point us toward true wisdom, true treasure? This analogy between wisdom and treasure, I don't think Job drew it into being. The metaphor is too perfect. I think Job simply documented a pre-existing, purposeful connection.

The Bible is full of realized metaphor. For example, Jesus calmed the storm and saved his followers from drowning (Luke 8:22-25). He also walked on troubled waters (Matthew 14:22-33). While these events were miraculous on their own, they had symbolic significance as well. Jesus demonstrated his authority not only over the sea, but also over the primordial chaos of creation. (Genesis 1:2; Job 9:8). The churning of the open sea is violent, unpredictable. At the beach, when we catch the fringes of the surf; out on boats, when the waves churn our stomach; we are meant to think about the forces of darkness, and the power of God to turn them to good. The sea is a metaphor, created for us to experience in space and time.

The sky, also, is given to us as a real-life picture of God. When I watch the sun set, filling the western sky with delicate pinks and purples, I often think of the beauty of God. He didn't have to share that with us. He didn't have to coordinate the receptors in our retinas with the colors in the sky. But he did! Creation is speaking to us! Or how about when the sky changes moods, and the clouds become angry. Who hasn't been a little frightened during a big storm, with the boom of thunder and the flash of lightning bolts? God is invisible, incomprehensible. And yet he created all these things to show us a little bit of himself.

Here is something even more delightful – we humans are a metaphor for God! God created us in his image, a living, embodied metaphor of our Creator (Genesis 1:27). He created us male and female, so that we could portray the eternal romance of Jesus and the Church (Ephesians 5:22-33). When we plan, and build, and speak, and love, we display God. More pointedly, when we fight discouragement, or lust, or anxiety, or selfishness, we are fighting the great enemies of God since the beginning of time.

All creation speaks of God, all the time. And this especially includes humankind. Experiencing life as metaphor can imbue even small, menial tasks with significance. When we are happy, we can rejoice sincerely in God's goodness and the goodness of his creation. When we are sad or angry, we can experience those emotions as a response to the brokenness of this world, which Christ has come to make whole.

May we recognize and portray God faithfully this week.

Job 28:12-28 (Lady Wisdom)

Job has painted a fantastically-detailed word picture of miners searching out hidden treasure. Then he reveals his punchline: "But where shall wisdom be found? And where is the place of understanding?" (v. 12). Like the falcons and the proud lions (vv. 7-8), we don't know the worth of wisdom, and we certainly don't know how to find it.

Job continues: *Wisdom, like buried treasure, exists far from the land of normal human life* (v. 4, 13). *Bring out a cosmic search light, and the Deep will say "not here!" The Sea will say "not here, either!" You can't buy wisdom, not for fine gold or dazzling jewels.* "The price of wisdom is above pearls." (v. 18) *It's exceedingly precious and rare.*

Again Job repeats his chorus: *Where is the place of wisdom? Its house is hidden from the living, even from the birds of the air. Death and Destruction have only heard rumors of it.* (vv. 20-22).

Yet God knows the way to wisdom. God doesn't need a search light, he sees to the ends of the earth, everything under the heavens. God knew wisdom from before time, when he weighed the wind, when he measured out the waters, when he instructed the lighting and the rain. By wisdom, God saw his creation; he declared it was good, he established it and searched it out. And God gave this key to man: "Behold, the fear of the Lord, that is wisdom, and to turn away from evil is understanding." (vv. 23-28).

Job's discourse on wisdom has an interesting parallel in Proverbs. Proverbs tells us that wisdom is better than gold, silver and jewels (Proverbs 8:10-11). Proverbs also confirms that wisdom requires humility, a proper fear of the Lord, and a hatred of evil (Proverbs 8:13).

But then comes the twist: In Proverbs, wisdom appears as a woman, brought forth by God as his companion before the great acts of creation. "When he established the heavens, I was there; when he drew a circle on the face of the deep... when he assigned to the sea its limit... then I was beside him, like a master workman" (Proverbs 8:27, 29). The Deep and the Sea cannot contain Wisdom, because she preceded them all. Not only that, Proverbs tells us that Wisdom rejoiced in God's world and especially in humankind (Proverbs 8:31).

In fact, Proverbs tells us that, while we must seek wisdom diligently (Proverbs 8:17), Wisdom also seeks us. Wisdom calls out from the heights, takes her stand at the town gates. "O simple ones, learn prudence; O fools, learn sense. . . Leave your simple ways, and live, and walk in the way of insight" (Proverbs 8:1-5, 9:6).

So which is it – is wisdom hidden, or is it plain? Do we have a shot at finding it? The stakes are tremendous: find wisdom, find life. But, if you hate wisdom and follow foolishness, you find death (Proverbs 8:35-36; 9:18).

Contrary to expectations, wisdom doesn't come from great intellect or great education. The Apostle Paul tells us that God has "made foolish the wisdom of the world... For the foolishness of God is wiser than men, and the weakness of God is stronger than men." (I Corinthians 1:20, 25). We can't find wisdom alone, but we can find it through Christ, who humbled himself through death and suffering (Ephesians 1:7-9). He is the Way. (John 14:6).

Job 29 (Happy Days)

Job has just finished his Ode to Wisdom, urging his listeners to fear God and turn away from evil. Job then moves on to describe his previous life, where he was a model of godly wisdom.

How I wish for the good old days, when God watched over me with kindness – and not with the unrelenting scrutiny I experience today! I could walk through darkness then, because God shone his light on my head. I was in my prime, the mighty God was with me, his council was near my tent. (vv. 2-5).

Out of all of Job's trials – sudden poverty, the death of his children, the disdain of his former friends – Job misses God's favor the most. This is his first and greatest sorrow, the (apparent) loss of fellowship with God. And isn't it also the unseen desire of all human hearts? We long for an intimate relationship with God, to experience the light of God's benevolence. Job is echoing the history of our ancestors, Adam and Eve, who once walked with God in the cool of the day, and then suddenly found themselves exiled from Eden.

It's interesting, as well, that Job describes himself as once privy to God's council (translated "friendship" in the ESV, v. 4). Job's current plight originated in a challenge placed by Satan before the council (1:6). Heaven remains focused on Job's response to suffering, although Job does not know it.

Job continues in a nostalgic vein: *My children surrounded me, my steps were well-oiled* [butter and oil being a sign of prosperity]. *I held a place of honor in public life. Young and old gave me deference, and even royalty stopped talking when I entered. I was blessed by everyone who heard me, I was approved by everyone who saw me.* (vv. 5-11).

And why was I held in such high regard? I was a champion of the poor and fatherless, the dying and the widow. I was clothed in righteousness and justice. "I was eyes to the blind and feet to the lame" (v.15). *I took fatherly care of the needy and the stranger. And I busted the chops of the bad guys. (vv. 12-17).*

Job lived an admirable life, marked by benevolence and justice. As we have seen, both God and Satan noticed Job's blameless life (1:8-9). The people also had great respect for Job, and it appears he had legal authority as a judge or arbitrator of disputes. This passage highlights the irony of Job's current condition, where he is cursed and seeks legal recourse against God, in vain.

In the old days Job was confident and secure: *I thought, "I shall die in my nest, and I shall multiply my days as the sand." (v. 18). I imagined myself a tree with a strong, spreading root system, refreshed by the evening dew. I imagined myself an archer with an ever-renewing bow. (vv. 19-20).*

People listened to me, they waited for my words and took them seriously. I was like the spring rain to them. I smiled on them, I could encourage them without becoming discouraged myself. I was like a king among his troops. Even in a time of mourning my words brought confidence and comfort. (vv. 21-25).

Although Job was righteous, his expectations were misplaced. His righteousness was not a guarantee of security, prosperity and a long life. In fact, this was Satan's very challenge: Would Job continue to be loyal to God, even if God's blessings were removed? Traditional wisdom, as we have seen from Job's friends, followed the "retribution principle": God rewards good behavior and punishes bad behavior. Job is learning that reality is more complex. God, in his sovereignty, uses both blessing and suffering for his purposes.

Job 30 (Stormy Times)

Job breaks from his nostalgic reverie. The contrast between past and present is stark. In this riches-to-rags story, are we even talking about the same person?

Job begins: *Elders and princes used to wait for my words. And now, even the rabble laughs at me. Young thugs – I would not have hired their fathers as farm hands. A bunch of useless and weak men, they have nothing;* "they gnaw the dry ground by night in waste and desolation" (v. 3); *they scavenge leaves and roots for food. They are cast out of society like a bunch of criminals. Homeless, they squat in ditches and caves; they huddle together in the bushes and bray like donkeys. SOBs and bastards, all of them! Yet they are the ones mocking me; when they see me, they spit and walk to the other side of the road.* (vv. 1-10).

Job gives an extended description of the dregs of society. Imagine skid row in Los Angeles. And yet these sketchy characters are higher on the social scale than Job. These good-for-nothing youths heighten Job's sense of suffering, but they are not the cause of it. Here Job points the finger at God: God has "loosed his cord" (v. 11). The image is of an archer, whose bow is unstrung and useless. Job has lost the respect of the people because God has humbled him.

Job describes the actions of the mob against him: they rise up, they trip his feet, they block and break his path, "they promote my calamity" (v. 13), they come against him like crashing waves. Job is unable to walk or even stand. "Terrors are turned upon me," says Job (v. 15). His honor has gone up in the whirlwind, and his prosperity has flown away like the clouds.

Are Job's tormentors acting alone, or has someone sent them? We have heard similar language before. In chapter 18, Bildad speaks of personified evil: Terror and Calamity chasing after the doomed man, causing him to stumble and perish (18:11-14). In chapter 19, Job attributes similar activity to God, blocking his path and breaking him down (Job 19:8-12). So is Job being persecuted by foolish men, by the forces of evil, or by God himself? The glittering truth is that God uses the free will of both humans and evil spirits to accomplish His good purposes (Romans 8:28). But this is difficult to see in the middle of the storm.

Job is drained and pained, inside and out. *My soul is poured out because of affliction. The pain in my bones keeps me up at night. My skin is disfigured and chafes me around the neck. And that is nothing compared with the thought that You, God, have abandoned me. Not only do you ignore my cries for help, you persecute me with your own mighty hand, tossing me like a rag doll in a hurricane. I despair of my life.* (vv. 16-23).

The pounding of stormy waves is an excellent metaphor for suffering. Buffeted from every side, our striving leads only to exhaustion. I remember thinking, perhaps God has me in his rock tumbler, to smooth out my harsh edges. But God is more precise than that. His goal is not sea glass, but the brilliance of diamond, cut by his expert hand (Revelation 21:11).

Job's thoughts spiral downward; he ruminates on his reversal of fortune. *When I was prosperous, I heard the cry of the poor and needy. I wept with them!* "But when I hoped for good, evil came, and when I waited for light, darkness came." (v. 26). *My guts are in turmoil, my skin blackened; I am consumed with fever. When I cry for help, people treat me like jackals in the desert. Sadness is my only song.* (vv. 29-31). At least for now, the comforter has become the mourner.

Job 31:1-12 (Portrait of a Saint)

In chapter 31, Job makes a strong declaration of innocence. Although Job's friends have urged him to repent, Job refuses to make a false confession – for this would be a sin in itself. In this passage, we gain insight into Job's concept of righteousness. Whether God chooses to bless him or curse him, Job will not give up his moral compass.

Job starts with the declaration, "I have made a covenant with my eyes; how then could I gaze at a virgin [or young woman]?" (v. 1). Job doesn't pull any punches -- lustful looking is first on his list of sins! Job knows how our eyes so easily lead us astray (1 John 2:16). In today's visual culture, where screens with beautiful women constantly entice us, Job's testimony is striking. Yet Jesus himself confirmed the need to guard our eyes: looking, by itself, can be adulterous. Jesus went on to issue the brutal challenge, "If your right eye causes you to sin, tear it out and throw it away." (Matthew 5:27-30).

Why so serious about the eyes? According to Job – and Jesus -- our eyes can jeopardize our eternal inheritance. "What would be my portion from God above and my heritage from the Almighty on high?" (v. 2). Job has respect for the all-seeing, all-knowing God. Job instinctively clings to the principle that God will execute justice – even while suffering as an innocent man himself.

Job then begins a series of oaths. These oaths contain curses, some implied and some explicit: "If I have done evil thing X, then let horrible thing Y happen to me." For example: *If I have walked in falsehood and deceit, or if my heart has turned from the right path, then let the work of my hands go to others. In fact, let whatever has grown for me be pulled up by the roots!* (vv. 5-8). Here we see echoes of the Psalms, which repeatedly urge us to walk the path of obedience to God (ex. Psalm 1:1; Psalm 23:3; Psalm 119:1-3). Job is fixed on this narrow way of righteousness; he would rather lose all the fruits of his labors than take one false step.

Job continues: *If my heart has coveted my neighbor's wife and led me into adultery, then let my wife serve another man, and let other men have sex with her. For adultery is a heinous crime, a burning fire from hell that would burn my house to the roots.* (vv. 9-12). This point is quite graphic. Some commenters have criticized Job for calling down a curse on his own wife. Yet in a traditional, patriarchal society (and even in our own society), a wife who sleeps with other men brings terrible shame to her husband. If such a curse were to land on Job's wife, it would not land on her alone.

In today's permissive society, with no-fault and no-judgment divorce, we can all give examples of families burned to the ground by a cheating husband. The wife and kids are also burn victims. Proverbs reinforces the image of adultery as a burning fire: "Can a man carry fire next to his chest, and his clothes not be burned?" (Proverbs 6:27). Job knows that the eyes pull the heart (v. 1, 7), and the heart pulls the feet and hands (v.9), resulting in sin and destruction. For this reason Job watches his eyes, his heart, his feet and his hands carefully.

Although Job was a rich and powerful man in his prime (chapter 29), his declaration of innocence is not about virtue-signaling for popular approval. We can all give examples of rich and powerful people, worshipped by the public, but who lack personal integrity and fail their families. In contrast, Job was faithful in his private life and desired righteousness from his heart. God's statement from the first chapter still rings true: "there is none like [Job] on earth, a blameless and upright man, who fears God and turns away from evil" (1:8).

Job 31:13 – 46 (The SJW Patriarch)

As we have seen, in chapter 31 Job swears a lengthy oath of innocence. His first two oaths relate to personal integrity: he has not lied, he has not lusted. And now Job turns to broader issues of justice. *If I have ignored the complaint of my servants, how could I answer God when he rises to their aid? The same God fashioned us both in our mothers' wombs.* (vv. 13-15). We know Job lived in a traditional, patriarchal society that included household servants. Yet Job did not abuse his position of authority. Job is certain God cares about those at the bottom of the food chain. And God will hold Job accountable if his servants have any complaints!

Today this passage sounds quaint, if not outright offensive. It's helpful to remember that the Bible records history truthfully, including the existence of fallen social systems like slavery and polygamy. Many of the great biblical heroes owned both slaves and concubines. Yet Job teaches us that, in the midst of such systems, it is still possible to think rightly and live a righteous life. Job recognizes that he and his slaves, both male and female, share a common humanity. We see in Job's speech the seeds of equality that would eventually spread to free the slaves, thousands of years later.

Next Job addresses the plight of the poor: *If I have been stingy with the poor; or denied the desires of the widow; or failed to share food with the orphan; or allowed the needy to go unclothed – if I have raised my hand and taken advantage of the fatherless, then let my arm fall useless and broken.* (vv. 16-23).

Job's compassion for the poor took place on a remarkably personal level. Job gave the fatherless his own "morsel" of food (v. 17). He treated the destitute like his own family members (v. 18). He clothed the poor with the fleece of his own sheep (v. 20). Later, we see that Job opened the doors of his own house to the traveler (v. 32) and filled the hungry with meat from his own livestock (v. 31). Job did not donate money to some far-away cause, or call for more government programs. Instead, Job observed and responded to the need in front of his own eyes. Job's dedication to social justice cost him directly.

And what was Job's motivation? Nothing less than the majesty and fear of God (v. 23). Before his trials, Job was a wealthy man. And yet, he was careful not to make wealth an idol: *If I have trusted in gold; or rejoiced in my great wealth – if the splendor of the sun and moon has enticed me to worship them – this would be an offense deserving punishment, for I would have been false to God in heaven.* (vv. 24-28). Job knows that God is the source of all blessing, the creator of gold, sun and moon. Job is careful to worship God alone, and not mere created things. This is at the heart of Job's service to others.

Job's code of ethics seems almost New Testament. Job is not a legalist, he is not simply following a set of detailed behavioral regulations. No, Job is concerned about the heart. He diligently guards his heart from lust and deceit. He has sincere, sacrificial compassion for the needy. Even though Job has enemies, he does not curse them, he is not happy to see them ruined (vv. 29-30). Job is foreshadowing the virtues preached by Christ in the Sermon on the Mount (Matt. 5:43-45).

Because Job fears God, he has not hidden sin in his heart. This enables him to live a public life, without fear of contempt from others (vv. 33-34). Skipping to the end of the chapter, Job seals his social justice bona fides with a concern for the land itself: *If I have mistreated my land or its workers, causing its furrows to "weep together," let thorns and stinkweed grow instead of grain.*

What does it mean to be righteous? Job's discourse is fascinating and demonstrates God's concern for our hearts most of all. Job's use of oaths is also curious – a topic for next time.

Job 31:35-37 (The Legal Challenge)

Job has sworn his innocence, and in the process we have received a crash course in ethics. Job was loyal to God in thought and deed, publicly and privately, with no regard for worldly status or personal gain. Ordinarily, a person's self-description would be suspect. But here we know, from the beginning of the story, that God himself considers Job uniquely upright (1:8). In fact, Job has been chosen for testing precisely because of his righteousness, although Job does not realize it.

Let's step back and take a look at the big picture. Job has lost everything – his fortune, his family, and his health. Job has spent the past 28 chapters lamenting and trying to process his suffering, with the "help" of his three friends. The friends hold to a traditional view of how the world works, sometimes called the "retribution principle." If you do what is right, things will go well for you. If things are not going well for you, well, you must have done something wrong. When reality does not fit with their worldview, the friends change reality. Job is suffering, therefore Job must have done something wrong.

Job holds fast to his integrity, as God noted (2:3). Job is not willing to "speak deceitfully for God" (13:7-8), to engage in wrong-headed apologetics by a false confession of guilt. At the same time, Job can't see the way out of his situation. He cycles between accusing God of injustice (9:17, 22-24) and longing for renewed friendship with his Creator (14:15; 29:4-5). Job shouts into the night: "TALK TO ME, GOD!"

Job 13:3, 22: "But I would speak to the Almighty, and I desire to argue my case with God... Then call, and I will answer; or let me speak, and you reply to me."

Job 23:3-4: "Oh, that I knew where I might find him, that I might come even to his seat! ... I would know what he would answer me and understand what he would say to me."

Periodically, Job has glimpses of hope. There must be a witness, an advocate for him in heaven (Job 16:19). There must be a Redeemer who will open the way for Job to see God (19:25-27). But the immediacy of his suffering keeps pulling Job into despair. Finally, Job has nothing to lose. In chapter 31, Job lays everything on the table before God.

Job declares: "Is not calamity for the unrighteous, and disaster for the workers of iniquity? Does he not see my ways and number all my steps?" (31:3-4). *OK God, you see everything. You know I have done nothing to deserve this suffering. Your reputation is on the line.* Job goes on to declare his innocence with an oath, calling down self-curses if he is lying. Job is trying to force God's hand: "DO SOMETHING, GOD!"

Job boldly summons God to court: "Here is my signature! Let the Almighty answer me!" (31:35). He goes further: "Oh, that I had the indictment written by my adversary [i.e., God]! Surely I would carry it on my shoulder; I would bind it on me as a crown." (31:35-36). Job's bravery has gone beyond the point of ridiculousness. He tells God, "put it in writing," so that Job can fashion it into a paper party hat!

Job knows it is a fool's errand to call God into court. God is stronger and a master debater. Plus God is the one who wrote the rules in the first place (9:19-20). But Job has exhausted all other avenues for satisfaction. Even if God slays him, Job wants an audience with the Almighty. He wants to see God face-to-face. (13:15-16).

Strangely, God is not offended by this challenge. In fact, God will be pleased to answer Job's request – in his own good time.

Job 32 (Fart Jokes)

In Chapter 31, Job issued a daring challenge – calling down curses on himself, demanding that God appear in court. The three friends realize Job has doubled down; he refuses to apologize and admit his misery is his own fault. So the friends stop talking (32:1).

We know that, in due time, God will respond to Job's cry (chs. 38-41). But before we reach those heights, we have a most rude interruption (chs. 32-27). Some guy we have never heard of, Elihu the son of Barachel the Buzite, of the family of Ram, butts in. Eli-who?

Elihu doesn't say "Excuse me, may I have a word?" No, Elihu is angry. He is angry at Job, "because he justified himself rather than God," and he is angry at the three friends, "because they had found no answer, although they had declared Job to be in the wrong." (v. 2-3). For good measure, the text tells us for the fourth time, Elihu "burned with anger." (v. 5).

It appears Elihu was eavesdropping on the entire conversation. However, because Elihu was "young in years," (vv. 4, 6) he waited for his elders to finish talking first. This was customary in Job's patriarchal society. But now Elihu seems to be changing his mind about the value of age: *I was afraid to speak; isn't wisdom supposed to come with age? But no, it is God's spirit that gives understanding. It's not only the old who are wise.* (vv. 7-9).

Age and experience have tremendous value. There are many things I wish I could go back and tell my younger self! But thinking back, these are all things that I have learned with the help of the Holy Spirit. Wisdom is not an automatic "pass go, collect $200." You don't grow wiser just by circling the sun another year.

Wisdom comes from God and from his word, and these are available to both young and old. According to the psalmist, "I have more understanding than all my teachers, for [God's] testimonies are my meditation. I understand more than the aged, for I keep

[God's] precepts." (Psalm 119:99-100). Jesus took this concept to the extreme when he said, "unless you turn and become like children, you will never enter the kingdom of heaven." (Matthew 18:3). Children have almost no life experience, and yet Jesus says the perspective of a child is necessary for heaven. So while it is good to honor those who are older, and to learn from them, no human has a monopoly on wisdom.

Emboldened by his anger, Elihu declares it is time for a new perspective: "[Job] has not directed his words against me, and I will not answer him with your speeches." (v. 14). Elihu sees himself as a neutral third party, perhaps responding to Job's plea for a mediator (v. 9:33). Elihu promises that he will not show bias or use flattery – he doesn't know how (vv. 21-22). Indeed, Elihu's speeches are bombastic and repetitive, without the nuance and high poetry of Job and his friends.

Take how Elihu describes himself: "For I am full of words; the spirit within me constrains me. Behold, my belly is like wine that has no vent; like new wineskins ready to burst. I must speak, that I may find relief." We have talked about fermentation as metaphor. Elihu's thoughts have fermented and swollen his belly. Job and his friends have referred to each other as wind bags (16:3, 15:2), but Elihu makes the joke explicit. A fart joke.

I guess age does make a difference with some things.

Job 33 (Behold!)

Behold! says Elihu. *Listen to me, I'm talking now!* As we saw from the last chapter, Elihu is very eager to talk. He tells Job and his friends to "Behold!" six times in chapter 33 alone – one commentator refers to it as a "verbal tic." Again, Elihu is young and not a polished speaker like the others. Yet, as we will see, in some ways Elihu comes closer to the truth about God and suffering.

I am speaking from a clean conscience and a sincere heart. My life is animated by God's Spirit. Here, Elihu echoes Job's claim that "the spirit of God is in my nostrils." (Job 27:3). This is a reference to God's creation of human beings. The first man, Adam, was "born" when God formed him from the ground, then breathed into his nostrils the breath of life (Genesis 2:7). By analogy, all humans are given life by God's Spirit at birth. Jesus goes one step further, by saying that Christians must be reborn by a special indwelling of the Holy Spirit. (John 3:5). But in this case, it seems Elihu is simply claiming that he has the same breath of God as Job and his friends, and that he has the same right to speak as they do.

In fact, Elihu may see himself as the answer to Job's prayers. In chapter 9:32-33, Job complains that God "is not a man, as I am, that I might answer him, that we should come to trial together." But here, Elihu reassures Job: *I am here, I am listening, I am human – "pinched off from a piece of clay" just like you. You don't need to fear me, I am not going to press you.* (vv. 6-7).

It turns out Elihu was listening closely to Job's speeches. He quotes Job back to Job: *I heard you say you are "pure" and "clean." I heard you complain that God nonetheless has come against you as an enemy, that God has trapped you and scrutinized you.* (vv. 8-11). Although Job did not claim to be completely without sin, he did claim to be a righteous man, suffering innocently (see chapter 31). And Job certainly did claim God was treating him as an enemy (19:6-12).

Elihu does not mince words: *You're wrong Job! Don't you recognize God is greater than man? Why are you fighting him, complaining that he doesn't answer you? God speaks to people in his own ways. For example, God can speak in dreams and night visions, terrifying men with warnings to turn them from their bad deeds. Thus God saves people from the downfall of pride, saves their soul from the pit, saves their life from death.* (vv. 12-18).

It is true that God sometimes speaks in dreams. For example, God warned the wise men and Joseph in a dream, to protect the baby Jesus from Herod (Matthew 12-13). God warned Pilate's wife in a dream that Jesus was an innocent man (Matthew 27:19). And there are many other examples of dreams in the Bible. Interestingly, Eliphaz spoke of a terrifying night vision in his first speech (4:12-21). However, the spirit in Eliphaz's dream was accusatory and did not seem to have the best interests of humans in mind. Elihu is speaking of dreams that, while scary, lead to repentance and restoration.

Elihu notes that God speaks in other ways as well, including rebuke through pain: aching bones, loss of appetite, wasted flesh, up to the point of death. (vv. 19-22). Job has experienced just this type of severe pain. Elihu claims that Job's suffering is God speaking to him. And at the very darkest point, when the suffering person is finally ready to hear the truth, God sends an angel or messenger to preach hope and call the person to repentance. (v. 23). Perhaps Elihu sees himself as that kind of spokesperson for Job.

As described by Elihu, the angelic messenger declares deliverance: *I have found a ransom! Let the man who suffers be restored to youthful vigor. Let him pray to God, and let God accept him. Let him admit his sin and sing of God's redemption. Let him look upon the light. Behold, Job, God is speaking to you!* (vv. 24-33).

Job 34:1-9 (Too harsh?)

When Elihu was first introduced, I had high hopes. Sure, he is younger and less polished than Job and his three friends (32:9). But we know God often uses the foolish to shame the wise (1 Corinthians 1:20). And sure, his eagerness to speak is somewhat off-putting: "Listen to me! Listen to me!" (basically, all of chapter 32). But Elihu seemed to recognize his common humanity with Job (33:7), and he seemed to offer hope for redemption (33:23-28). Elihu also seemed to deviate from the rigid perspective of Job's other three friends, who saw Job's suffering as simple punishment for sin. According to Elihu, God uses suffering for a redemptive purpose, to bring us back to him (33:29-30).

So I can't help but feel disappointed by Elihu's words to Job in this chapter. He seems to fall into the pattern of the other three friends, kicking a good man while he is down. I have to remind myself that, while Job was righteous, he wasn't perfect. And we know from the introduction to Elihu's speeches that he was angry at Job "because he justified himself rather than God." (32:2). Job has said some heavy things about God, and Elihu is eager to defend God's justice.

Elihu begins characteristically: Listen to me! Then he makes a proposal. Job has repeatedly stated the rightness of his case, to the point of challenging God to a legal hearing (31:35). Elihu wants to take up that challenge, to consider Job's case. "For the ear tests words as the palate tastes food. Let us choose what is right; let us know among ourselves what is good." (vv. 3-4).

Elihu summarizes his understanding of Job's legal case. "For Job has said, 'I am in the right, and God has taken away my right.'" (v. 5). *Job claims that God has wounded him unjustly, so that Job has been made out to be a liar.* (v. 6). This is exactly the position that makes Elihu angry. With the apostle Paul, Elihu seems to be saying, "Let God be true though every one were a liar." (Romans

3:4). If Elihu has to choose between God and Job, he is going to choose God. Elihu responds harshly to Job's position: "what man is like Job, who drinks up scoffing like water, who travels in company with evildoers and walks with wicked men?" (vv. 7-8).

According to Elihu, Job claims that "It profits a man nothing that he should take delight in God." (v. 9) As Christians we know that delighting in God is everything, man's highest purpose. So, of course, it is grave heresy to claim that delighting in God is unprofitable and worthless. But did Job really believe this?

Certainly Job flirted with the idea that God's justice is arbitrary (9:22, 21:17-18). Job also noted, as do other Biblical writers, that the wicked often prosper in this life (24:1-12). Yet even in his darkest hour, Job's heart still belonged to God. Job recognized God's loving care in fashioning him (10:8-12). Job waited fervently for God's call (14:14-15). Job treasured God's word and recognized the priceless value of God's wisdom (12:11-12, all of chapter 28). Job longed for restored friendship with God (29:2-5). Even while his body decayed, Job looked forward in faith to seeing God with his own eyes (19:25-27).

So I don't think Job believed "it profits a man nothing that he should take delight in God." In fact, in one of Job's speeches, he puts similar words in the mouth of the wicked. While the wicked go about fat and happy, singing and dancing, they say to God, "What is the Almighty, that we should serve him? And what profit do we get if we pray to him?" (21:15). Job then specifically rejects this perspective, saying "The counsel of the wicked is far from me" – even though they prosper (21:16).

Although Job's heart is in the right place, there may yet be truth in Elihu's words. Perhaps Job's unending sorrow has revealed lingering dross. Perhaps Job's faith needs further refinement.

Job 34:10-37 (God Is Great, God Is Good)

At the very beginning of his trial, Job states his willingness to receive from God's hand whatever God is pleased to give, good or bad (1:21, 2:10). Yet as his suffering lingers, Job sees God against him, as an enemy (9:17-18, 19:8-12). Job is bitter toward God -- and this makes Elihu angry. Elihu, young and bombastic, tries to change Job's perception of God.

Listen up, you so-called wise men! God cannot do wrong. He will repay men according to their deeds. (v. 10-12). This sounds a lot like the retribution principle spouted repeatedly by Eliphaz, Bildad and Zophar. Yet there is truth in Elihu's words: God can't do wrong, and people will be judged for their deeds. (2 Corinthians 5:10). At the same time, we should not expect perfect justice to be played out in this fallen world. God will make all things right *in the end.*

Elihu continues his defense of God. *God has the whole world in his hands, and no one is the boss of him. If God merely sucks in his breath, all living creatures would perish. Listen up, you so-called wise men! God is ruler over all. Will you condemn the one who judges kings? God does not favor the rich and powerful, for all people are equally the work of his hands.* (vv. 13-20).

God watches each step of every man. There is no darkness so deep that the wicked can hide from God (vv. 21-22). *Evildoers will die unexpectedly, and not by human hands* (vv. 20, 25). *God made us and can unmake us just as quickly. God sees the wicked taking their own path, he hears the cry of the poor and the oppressed, and he acts. He strikes down the wicked where everyone can see it* (vv. 26-28).

Elihu alludes to Job's request for a hearing before God (9:32, 14:13, 31:35). "For God has no need to consider a man further, that he should go before God in judgment." (v. 23). *God doesn't need investigations – he knows everything already.* Elihu implies that the hearing Job wants is useless.

Elihu also chides Job for complaining about God's silence (see, chapter 23). "When he [God] is quiet, who can condemn? When he hides his face, who can behold him, whether it be a nation or a man?" (v. 29). *God speaks when he pleases, shows himself to whom he pleases. And God has his purposes in silence, both for individuals and for nations.* Verse 30 is not entirely clear, but it could be referring to the fact that wicked rulers, especially, should not expect the favor of seeing God.

The next several verses (31-33) are also somewhat difficult to understand. It seems that Elihu is holding out hope of repentance, as he did in chapter 33. *What if a person accepts God's discipline and turns from doing wrong? What if a person asks God to teach him how to sin no more? How will God respond? You, Job, have the ability to reject or choose what is right; no one can do that for you.*

Elihu ends with a final critique of Job. *Wise men will agree with me that Job speaks without knowledge, and his words are without insight.* (v. 35). We know that Job's understanding was incomplete, since God makes the same comment (38:2) and Job ultimately agrees (42:3). Job in his suffering certainly did not have the big picture.

Yet Elihu's criticism goes further. *If Job were put on trial (as he has requested), he would not be found righteous. Job answers like wicked men, rebels against God's discipline, speaks against God himself.* (vv. 36-37). Elihu's zeal for God's reputation is admirable. But at the same time, Elihu speaks too harshly against Job, not recognizing that Job is God's servant (2:3). Perhaps Elihu's knowledge, also, is incomplete.

Job 35 (What does it matter?)

Elihu is still angry with Job and his friends. The friends have argued a simplistic, cause-and-effect relationship between humanity and God: if a man acts righteously, God will bless him. This gives people a certain power to manipulate God. We think, I did this good thing, therefore God owes me one. And Job probably held to this belief in the past. Job probably expected God's favor as long as he played by the rules.

Then the unexpected happened: Job's life fell apart, though he was innocent. Job's friends urged him to confess his secret sin, so God would restore him. But Job held fast to his integrity. Job refused to make a false confession – not to manipulate God or even to protect God's reputation. (And God's reputation was on the line, just in a different way than Job could understand.) As Job cries out to God in physical and mental anguish, the question emerges: What does God owe Job? How is Job any better off for being righteous?

On this point Elihu continues his diatribe. "Do you think this to be just? Do you say, 'It is my right before God,' that you ask 'What advantage have I? How am I better off than if I had sinned?'" (vv. 2-3). Elihu responds to his own question: *God owes you nothing! Look up, see how the clouds are so much higher than you. Sin and righteousness are purely human concerns. Your sin can't hurt God, and your righteousness doesn't obligate him either.* (vv. 5-8).

Objectively, it is true that our puny actions can't hurt or help God in any way. As Paul states, "who has given a gift to [the Lord], that he might be repaid?" (Romans 11:35). God in heaven has no need of our earthly sacrifices, and we can't give anything to him that didn't come from him in the first place. But, yet - Job's story itself informs us that one person's choices do matter. In his wager with

Satan, God staked his reputation on the line with Satan: will Job curse God under testing?

Each choice between good and evil is a re-enactment of the Fall. Adam's rebellion against God had consequences; the sin of our first parents was imbued with terrible meaning. And God still includes us, weak as we are, in his plan to end evil and re-make the world. Our response to suffering is part of the cosmic drama, a "spectacle to the world, to angels, and to men." (1 Corinthians 4:9). So although our choices don't obligate God, he cares about them deeply.

Elihu continues: *Lots of people are oppressed and suffer, calling out for help. But they don't recognize God as their Maker, the source of music, wisdom and meaning. God doesn't answer the empty cries of proud and evil men.* (vv. 9-13). Job has wondered why God remains silent in the face of oppression (ex. 24:12). Elihu seems to say that not all cries for help are the same. We must cry out in humility, not proud indignation.

Elihu seems to put Job in the category of those that should not expect an answer from God. Elihu says to Job: *You say you don't see him, you have put your case in front of him, and you are waiting for a response. But your words have not prompted God to action -- God appears to be ignoring injustice. For this reason your talk is empty and without knowledge.* (vv. 14-16).

Again, Elihu speaks some words that are true, but not the whole truth. In his distress, Job does speak words "without knowledge" – God says so himself (38:2). Yet we will see that God does hear Job's cry, and he does answer. Job's suffering, and his plea for help, matter greatly to God.

Job 36:1-13 (Elihu the Jerk?)

I have to admit, I am having trouble with the Elihu speeches. In the words of one commentator, they are "bombastic" and "repetitive." Job and his three friends spoke beautifully, even when the subject matter was brutal. But Elihu is just not as fun to read. His poetry is stilted rather than lyrical.

Elihu's role is also enigmatic. The prose narrative tells us that Job spoke rightly about God (for the most part), while Job's three friends spoke wrongly (Job 42:7). But the text does not tell us how to think about Elihu, who is not mentioned outside of his speeches. Some commentators lump Elihu with the three friends, assuming that his perspective is in the same tradition and deserves the same condemnation.

More liberal commentators speculate that the Elihu speeches were added later, an intrusion by a lesser scribe. But my belief is that all Scripture, including the Elihu speeches, was given for our instruction and growth (2 Timothy 3:16-17). For this reason, I am trying to be charitable toward Elihu. After all, he states up front that he is younger than the others (32:6). Perhaps Elihu suspects that his oratorical powers are not up to the standards of the older speakers. He does seem self-conscious, continually demanding that the others listen (ex. 32:17-20, 33:1-5, 31-33, 34:2, 10, 16, 35:4, 36:2-4).

And his timing is interesting. Elihu speaks right after Job's final words, and before the climactic appearance of the Lord. Is he preparing the way for the Lord in some fashion? We know that John the Baptist made a crude figure, dressed in rough clothes and eating locusts with honey (Mark 1:6). Yet John was the messenger preparing the way for Christ (Luke 7:24-28). Perhaps this is true of Elihu in some way. John Piper believes the Elihu speeches have unique value. And at least one author changed his mind about Elihu between writing two books about Job!

To summarize Elihu's speeches thus far, he has made several points that diverge from the three friends. First, God can use suffering for redemptive purposes, to bring people back from the edge of the pit (33:12-28). Second, God is just, and it is not our place to question him (34:12, 23, 29). Third, God doesn't need us, and we can't force him to act on our timetable (35:8, 14). It's all very humbling.

Which makes it ironic that Elihu himself comes across as quite arrogant. In Chapter 36, he begins: "Bear with me a little, and I will show you, for I have yet something to say on God's behalf." (v. 2). Elihu claims to be speaking for God! He goes on to say, "For truly my words are not false; one who is perfect in knowledge is with you." (v. 4). Is Elihu really claiming to be *perfect* in knowledge? It seems he has gotten out over his skis this time.

Elihu begins his final speech: *Behold, God is mighty, yet he does not despise humankind. He cares for the afflicted, not the wicked. He watches over the righteous, and he sets kings on their thrones, exalted.* (vv. 5-7). Elihu then picks up his theme that sometimes, the righteous do suffer. *If righteous kings do suffer, held hostage by their affliction, God lets them know that they have been acting pridefully. God opens their ears and calls them to repentance. Then they can either listen and complete their years in prosperity, or refuse to listen and perish, ignorant.* (vv. 8-12).

Again, Elihu emphasizes the redemptive aspect of suffering, and how God uses it to discipline us. Elihu also emphasizes the choice we have, to either listen or continue in rebellion, similar to his speech in 34:33. Although Elihu himself is somewhat pompous, he continues to emphasize the sin of pride. Could it be that Job is harboring pride in his heart, and God is using Elihu to point it out?

Job 36:13 – 33 (Don't Long for the Night)

Elihu continues his admonitions toward Job. Again, while his delivery is abrupt, Elihu's words are more nuanced than those of the three friends. *Your actions do not bind God, who is sovereign; in fact, suffering may just be his warning to you.*

Picking up in verse 13, Elihu describes the difference between righteous and unrighteous responses to suffering. *When the godless suffer, they just get angry. They don't ask for help when God restrains them. Instead, their lives are short and degenerate. But for the righteous, God uses suffering for their deliverance. If you hear God's voice, he will lead you out of distress into a wide open space, a place of feasting.* (vv. 13-16).

Watch out Job! I can see that you are seized by indignation. Your sense of justice has been offended. Don't let your anger lead you into scoffing, where even a great ransom won't be able to deliver you. You can't save yourself by your own efforts, not with all the force of your strength. Elihu warns: *Don't let your suffering cause you to sin.* (vv. 17-19).

We know that suffering, while painful, can be a valuable learning experience. We talk about the "school of hard knocks," which is part of becoming a mature adult. Going deeper, God also uses suffering to conform our character to the character of Christ. But suffering doesn't always have a positive spiritual outcome. We can resist the work of God, we can allow anger to fester, we can turn to sinful escapes. We can even fantasize about death, as Job does in chapter 3. Elihu reminds us, *Don't long for the night. Watch out. Don't turn to sin for relief.* (vv. 20-21).

So how do we stop wallowing? How do we get out of our suffering-induced funk? Elihu encourages us to fix our eyes on God, to praise his greatness. *God is exalted, there is no teacher like him. And he has no teacher; no one can tell God "no." So let's sing God's praises, which are visible to all people. God is outside time and space. Just look at his extraordinary power over the weather: drawing up the water drops in evaporation, then distilling them into rain, which the skies pour abundantly on mankind.* (vv. 22-28).

As I write, it is hurricane season. There is nothing like a big storm to let you know that you are not in charge. This weekend, my son was stranded at the Dallas airport, his connecting flight cancelled; my husband was unable to complete his many outdoor projects. What can we do in the face of a storm? For one, we can meditate on the attributes of God.

Elihu continues: *Who understands the spreading clouds, the thunder of God's battle cry? His lightning flashes to the sea floor. By such storms God executes judgment, yet he also waters the earth to give food. God commands the lightning; his presence is declared by the crash of thunder, so that even the cattle take notice.*

And what an amazing image! Clouds darken the sun, while lightning pierces the shadows. We are reminded of Psalm 139:11-12, where God's presence pursues the psalmist into dark places: "If I say, 'Surely the darkness shall cover me, and the light about me be night,' even the darkness is not dark to you; the night is bright as the day, for darkness is as light with you."

Christian brothers and sisters, don't long for the night. God's presence reaches the deepest darkness. You can't escape him, or his sovereign purposes for your suffering.

Job 37 (KA-BOOM)

When my oldest son was little, we lived in a high-rise apartment. My son's crib stood next to a large window. One evening, a huge electrical storm blew through town. The scene in the window rattled and flashed, and my son screamed bloody murder. Afterwards, he refused to sleep in that crib ever again.

Although Elihu is a grown man, he admits to being terrified by a great storm. He says, "my heart trembles and leaps out of its place." (v. 1). *Hear that thunder? It's the voice of God booming. And just look at God's special effects: lightning flashes from sky to ground. It's great, it's majestic, it's wondrous! And it's beyond our comprehension.* (vv. 1-5).

Thunder and lightning are meant to remind us of God, earthly signs of heavenly truth. When the Lord appeared to the prophet Ezekiel, he came with wind, and a great cloud, and lightning, and "the sound of many waters." Ezekiel's only possible response was to fall flat on his face. (Ezekiel 1). Elihu echoes this same awe; the storm he describes is likely raging as he speaks. In fact [spoiler alert], we are about to witness an appearance of the Lord, a theophany.

Elihu continues: *God speaks, and the snow and rain obey. People and animals obey as well: they retreat inside, shut the door, hibernate in their dens. Then comes the whirling blizzard, the icy breath of God, freezing the lakes fast. God himself loads the clouds; they accomplish his purposes by his guidance across the face of the earth. God uses the very weather to discipline, to provide for the land, to show his love.* (vv. 6-13).

At this point, the storm appears to subside. In the interlude, Elihu urges Job, and us: *Stop! Consider God's wonderful works! Do you know how he does it? How he commands the clouds, balancing their loads? God is perfect in knowledge. When the south wind comes, you can't even cool off your own clothes.* "Can you, like him, spread out the skies, hard as a cast metal mirror?" (v. 18). Compared with God's power over the weather, our own knowledge is pathetic and puny.

Finally, after six chapters, Elihu comes to his main point: rebuking Job for his repeated insistence on an audience with God. *So Job, teach me what a mere human could say to God. Our understanding is too dark. There's no way we could draw up our case, we would just be bumbling around. I wouldn't dare tell God to let me speak. I don't want to be swallowed up! And you shouldn't either!* (vv. 19-20).

Indeed, Job's final speech – probably the "last straw" that got Elihu riled up – was a challenge: "Let the Almighty answer me!" (31:35). Job knew God had the power to slay him, yet he longed to speak with him (13:3). Job even declared, "I will argue my ways to his face"! (13:15). Job had bizarre confidence – do we call it faith? – that God would put aside his advantage and pay attention to him (23:4-7). The problem was that Job didn't know where to find God (23:3).

Elihu tells Job to let that fantasy go. *When the clouds have passed, no one can look at the bright sun. Likewise, God dwells in golden splendor, on his holy mountain, clothed in awesome majesty. We can't find the Almighty. His power is great, it is against his nature to do anything but abundant righteousness.* "Therefore men fear him; he does not regard any who are wise in their own conceit." (v. 24).

Throughout the dialogue between Job and his friends, Job has been focused on himself and his suffering. Job's pride has been revealed. As Elihu reminds us, the cure for pride is to contemplate the greatness of the Creator. How could Job presume a response from God? And yet, God does respond.

Job 38:1-11 (Q & A)

The Greek philosopher Socrates taught his students by asking questions. Two thousand years later, when I was a law student, professors still used the "Socratic method." Even when I was prepared for class, my heart pounded every time the professor called my name. How much more terrifying to face questions from the living God?

Out of the whirlwind, the LORD answers Job. Job has been waiting for this a long time – 37 chapters, to be exact. From his place of suffering, Job has cursed the day of his birth (3:3-10). He has accused God of wounding him for no reason (9:17), and he has demanded that God explain himself, in writing (31:35). Lo and behold, God actually shows up.

God immediately puts Job on the hot seat: "Who is this that darkens counsel by words without knowledge?" (v. 2). Although Job has searched high and low for wisdom (28:12-22), his accusations against God demonstrate a lack of understanding. Job has clouded God's purposes with his doubts. And now it's time for God to set the record straight -- by asking questions. "Dress for action like a man; I will question you, and you make it known to me." (v. 3). *Pop quiz, are you ready?*

Question one: Where were you when I laid the foundation of the earth?

Question two: Who determined the earth's measurements? Who took measuring tape and confirmed its exact dimensions?

Question three: How were the footings of the earth secured?

Question four: Who laid the earth's cornerstone, "when the morning stars sang together and all the sons of God shouted for joy?"

C'mon, Job, you got this! (vv. 4-7).

God asks Job to consider the structure of the earth, carefully built according to divine blueprints. Actual stars sang for the groundbreaking ceremony. And all the members of God's spirit council shouted with wonder. Such is God's perfect rule over creation.

Bonus question: who set the limits for the sea? Genesis tells us that, in the beginning, the face of the earth was formless and covered with water (Genesis 1:2). God imposed order on primeval chaos, setting boundaries for the seas. Perhaps as a counter-point to Job cursing the day of his birth, God describes the sea as a big baby, bursting out from the womb. God tenderly swaddled the sea in fog, and placed it in a kind of playpen. "Thus far shall you come, and no farther, and here shall your proud waves be stayed." (v. 11).

Who talks to the seas that way? Certainly not Job. Only God can do that. The ocean waves, with all their power, are like children to him – he can silence them with a word. This is why Jesus could sleep in absolute peace on the boat, while his disciples screamed into the windstorm. "And he awoke and rebuked the wind and the raging waves, and they ceased, and there was a calm. He said to them, 'Where is your faith?' And they were afraid, and they marveled, saying to one another, 'Who then is this, that he commands even winds and water, and they obey him?'" (Luke 8:22-25).

Job, where is your faith?

Job 38:12-21 (Sunrise)

God has shown up, dramatically. He is providing an "answer" to Job's questions (v. 1), but it is not the answer that Job expects. God doesn't address Job's suffering directly – he barely mentions human beings at all. Instead, God points to his power and design in creation. Job is left to draw the appropriate inferences himself.

Picking up at verse 12, God continues his series of rhetorical questions: *Have you ever ordered up a sunrise, Job?* Every morning, without fail, the sun brings light and warmth to the earth. As its rosy glow creeps up from the horizon, the features of the earth become visible – like clay under a seal, or a garment being dyed (v. 14).

The orbit of the sun is both beautiful and functional. And it serves a moral purpose as well. God describes the dawn as picking up "the skirts of the earth" so that the wicked are "shaken out of it." (v.12). With the rising sun, the power of evil is broken (v. 15).

We know that evildoers love the dark. As Christ told Nicodemus, "For everyone who does wicked things hates the light and does not come to the light, lest his works should be exposed." (John 3:20). In fact, Job has bemoaned the evil deeds that take place during the night (24:13-17). This causes Job to question God's justice (24:12). But the sun's daily circuit confirms that God loves righteousness and hates wickedness. God defeats darkness every morning. And only God can do this. Job is not capable of ordering the natural or moral world in this way.

The Lord continues: *Oh Job? Have you walked in the depths of the sea?* Even today, perhaps only 5% of the ocean floor has been observed. According to worldatlas.com, "Little is known about the ocean floor as high water pressure, pitch black darkness, and extreme temperatures challenge exploration." The depths of the sea are also an echo of the depths of the grave. God asks Job again: *Have you even seen the outer gates of death?* (v. 17).

When Job wished for darkness and death (ch. 3), he was challenging God's good order of creation. God answers: *There is no corner of the physical or spiritual universe outside of my jurisdiction.* As the Psalmist writes: "Where shall I flee from your presence? If I ascend to heaven you are there! If I make my bed in the grave, you are there! If I take the wings of the morning and dwell in the uttermost parts of the sea, even there your hand shall lead me..." (Psalm 139:7-10). Morning and evening, birth and death, God holds them all in his hands.

God has more questions for Job: *Where do light and dark live? Can you lead them back to their proper homes? Surely you know, you must have been around back then!* (vv. 19-21). God is being sarcastic with poor Job. Of course Job can't control light or dark. But God can. Light and dark don't just happen randomly to God. God sees in the dark, and he is not blinded by the light (Psalm 139:12). He is the one who separated light from dark at the beginning, and gave them their names: Day and Night (Genesis 1:3-5).

Job's life took a dark turn overnight, and he can't seem to find his way back. But the God of both light and darkness promises: The sunrise is coming.

Job 38:22-38 (Secrets of the Universe)

Two framed photographs, souvenirs from a family vacation in Arizona, hang side-by-side in our bedroom. One photo captures – or tries to capture, I'm not a great photographer – the desert sunset, beautiful in oranges, yellows and dusky overtones. The other photo, titled NGC 1333, was taken by an astronomer at the Mt. Lemmon observatory. A reflection nebula located in the constellation Perseus, NGC 1333 spills over with twinkling stars and glowing cosmic dust. Clouds of earth and clouds of space, both speak hauntingly of mysteries beyond our understanding.

But not beyond God. Picking up in chapter 38, God continues to address Job: *So have you seen my stockpiles of snow and hail? You may have noticed, we have epic battles up here. And my ammo is well-supplied. I don't suppose you know the place where the light gets distributed? Or where the east wind gets scattered on the earth?* (vv. 22-24).

God is King of the natural order, in complete control of his creation. He has a place for everything, and everything in its place. The east wind, in particular, caused great trauma for Job – it came out of nowhere, collapsed the house of Job's oldest son, and killed all Job's children (1:19). But even that rogue wind was under God's control the entire time. God saw the wind leave its place of origin; it did not surprise him one bit.

So, Job, who cleft the channels from heaven to earth, opening a path for the rain and lightning? Who brings rain in deserted lands? Even there, grass springs forth (v. 25-27). God is subtly needling Job, letting him know that man is not the center of the universe. God alone brings rain and growth to the world, to pristine wilderness without human habitation. And he does this for his own reasons, unrelated to our human activity. The "retribution principle," where God is supposedly obligated to respond to our choices, has no place in the natural world.

Again God riffs on the weather: *Who fathered the rain? Who gave birth to ice and frost? How do the teeming waters – full of movement and chaos – freeze still and hard as stone?* God uses the metaphor of birth, again, as he did with the sea (vv. 8-11). The intimate language of birth is striking when applied to forces of nature. But even these seemingly-impersonal events are animated by the breath of God (37:10).

God throws an even wider scope: *How about the stars, Job? Can you conduct the Zodiac? Guide the path of the Big Dipper? Do you know "the ordinances of the heavens," and can you "establish their rule on the earth"?* (vv. 31-33). According to Genesis, God made the heavenly bodies on the fourth day of creation. In both a physical and metaphorical way, these guiding lights rule over the skies, telling us the time and season (Genesis 1:14-19). In our technological age, we think of the stars as fiery balls of gas. But God sees them singing and dancing through the sky (v. 7). God calls them by their given names – not some impersonal numbering system like NGC 1333 (Psalm 147:4). The distant heavens, like the earthly weather patterns, are alive with God's spirit.

God continues: *Can you speak to the clouds? Can you tip them over like a canteen, and satisfy the thirsty clods of dirt? Does the lightning follow your orders, and report back to you? Job, you searched for wisdom – just look at the clouds! Who numbers the clouds? Who tucks wisdom into human hearts?* (vv. 34-38).

Who indeed? It's God, the Master of the secrets of the universe.

Job 38:39 – 41 (The Zoo Keeper)

When John and I moved to the country, we were all excited to keep chickens. We found our feathered friends endlessly fascinating – the chirps and crows, the different personalities, the mating rituals. And there's nothing like farm-fresh eggs.

At the same time, keeping birds is a lot of work! John undertook great building projects: yard after yard of fencing, plus mobile and stationary coops. He also tried myriad feed and water systems. Sadly, our flocks suffered repeated attacks by possums, snakes, and wild dogs. Despite John's best efforts – which included a stakeout with night vision goggles -- our birds have been greatly reduced. We were not able to care for them perfectly.

Fortunately, God is not like us.

Back in our Job narrative, God has just finished describing his wise rule over the heavens. Actually – to be more accurate – God asked whether Job was competent to take charge of the ocean, the day and night, the snow and rain, the stars, the clouds. As we will see, Job has no response (40:5). And now, God turns his attention back to earth, to the animal kingdom. God calls out various creatures, mostly wild, and asks Job: can you care for these?

God asks: *Job – can you hunt prey for the lion? Can you satisfy their appetites, when they hide in the thickets?* (v. 38:39-40). God starts his parade of beasts with the lion. This makes sense; the lion is the undisputed king of the wild. Christ himself is called "Lion of Judah," king of God's people. Of course, as C.S. Lewis points out, lions are "not safe." The devil is described as a prowling, hungry lion (1 Peter 5:8). In his suffering, Job feared that God would hunt him like a lion (10:16).

Dangerous forces inhabit the natural world. God subtly reminds Job of the circle of life, nature red in tooth and claw, both majestic and savage. And – here is the point -- our God is lord of them all. God knows the secret lair of the fiercest beasts, and it is God who provides them with their food.

God continues: *And what about the ravens, when their chicks cry to God for help? Who feeds them?* The raven is a fairly large, common, dark-colored bird. Ravens eat almost anything, including carrion. For this reason, they were considered unclean in the Old Testament (Leviticus 11:13). The raven isn't particularly attractive, or melodic. In fact, ravens are considered something of a pest.

Yet even the raven is one of God's creatures. And God hears their cry for food. Interestingly, this is the same word that Job uses in his distress: "Behold, I cry out, 'Violence!' but I am not answered" (19:7). If God hears the cry of the pesky raven, he certainly hears the cry of his followers. This is exactly the point Christ made when he said, "Consider the ravens: they neither sow nor reap, they have neither storehouse nor barn, and yet God feeds them. Of how much more value are you than the birds!" (Luke 12:24).

God knows his creatures. God provides for his creatures. And these are the wild animals, the predators and pests of the world. They don't even taste good, or lay eggs for breakfast. God cares for them perfectly. It's good he is the cosmic zoo keeper, and not us.

By implication, God knows and cares for Job, and for his people today.

Job 39:1-18 (Wild Kingdom)

God continues quizzing Job on his knowledge of the animal kingdom: *Do you know when the mountain goats give birth? Do you count off the months of their pregnancy? Can you tell when it's time for their young to be delivered? And look how strong the young kids become; they will leave to start their own families.* (vv. 1-4).

We see here that God is pro-life, in its most general sense. While Job curses the day he was born (ch. 3), God oversees the birth of wild goats on the mountains. God likes to bring forth new life; he waits patiently while his creatures form in utero. And if God tends to wild animals in this way, how much more does he attend to human babies, made in his image? God also watches as new life becomes old, sustaining the cycle of reproduction through the generations.

God then asks: *What about the wild donkeys, who let them go free? I wanted the donkeys to run with abandon, so I gave the wastelands for their home. They scorn the noise of civilization, they refuse the orders of the cart-drivers. Instead, the donkeys range here and there over the mountains, searching out good green things to eat.* (vv. 5-8).

We see God is also pro-freedom. Job complains that God has hedged him in, caught him in a net, walled up his path (3:23, 19:6, 8). But God is not a prison guard. God gave Adam and Eve free will – which, unfortunately, they used to rebel against him, becoming slaves to sin. God then sent his Son to set the captives free (Isaiah 61:1, Luke 4:18). It gives God joy to see his creatures run free, even the jackasses.

The next stop on Job's safari trip? The wild ox. If that doesn't conjure any images in your mind, think about wild buffalo or bison on the prairies, before the pioneers arrived. God asks, *Will the wild ox serve you? Can you domesticate him, bind him to work your plow? He sure is strong. It sure would be useful to have him perform your labor. But can you really trust him to bring in your grain?* (vv. 9-12).

I think God is taunting Job a little bit here. An ox would make a great agricultural worker – provided it was cooperative. But taming the wild ox is an iffy proposition. Perhaps it could be done, but only after a lifetime of dangerous work, with multiple generations of breeding for friendliness and smaller size. The wild ox reminds us of our limitations. Sure, God gave humans responsibility to rule the animal kingdom (Genesis 1:26). But our rule is not absolute; it is a stewardship. Ultimately, creation does not serve us – it serves the Lord.

Next we have a surprise guest, the ostrich. *Take a look at the ostrich,* God says, *as she proudly flaps her wings. But they aren't the kind of feathers you can nestle into at night. She drops her eggs on the earth, doesn't bother trying to keep them warm. She doesn't think about the fact that some other creature might trample them. She treats her young cruelly, with no maternal instinct. Yes, I made her foolish. But when she rouses herself to run, she can laugh at the horse and rider.* (vv. 13-18).

The ostrich is rather ridiculous. I get the sense that, while the ostrich may laugh at the horse, God is also laughing at the ostrich. Some creatures are just like that. The tom turkeys on our farm are pretty funny, with droopy snoods covering their beaks, faces that flush deep red and purple, and gobble-gobble calls to each other. Perhaps God wants to show Job that he is pro-fun.

When tragedy strikes, we can forget important truths. God uses the animal kingdom to "show, not tell" Job what he is missing. With Job, may we remember the God who sustains life, freedom, and even fun.

Job 39:19-30 (War Horse)

My friend owns a horse farm on the other side of town. She gives lessons, performs at shows, and even hosts summer camps. I have a lot of respect for my friend, because horses require a lot of work; they are high maintenance animals.

And horses are impressive: tall and handsome, muscular and graceful. No wonder warriors throughout history chose to ride horses into battle. Up through World War I, the U.S. military relied heavily on horses. (Today we rely on tanks – practical, but not quite as regal).

Back in Job chapter 39, God continues his survey of the animal kingdom. With almost comedic timing, God turns from the ostrich to the war horse. *Job, do you give the horse his might? (v. 19). Do you give him his battle dress, the mane on his neck? Do you make him leap and paw the air? Do you give him his majestic and terrifying snort?*

Look at the horse's strength and bravery. He laughs at fear, he is eager to meet the weapons of war. He carries quivers of arrows, flashing spears and javelins. He races across the ground in fierce anger. When the trumpet sounds, he shouts for joy (v. 25). He lives for the smell of battle, the thunder of captains and troops shouting.

All this begs the question, who is the mysterious rider of this majestic horse? Whose arrows, spears and javelins rattle on his back? Who directs his movement? Whose battle is he fighting, anyway? God leaves Job, and us, to read between the lines, to ponder the negative space in this word-picture.

Job is no match for this horse, even though God has ordered Job to "dress for action like a man!" (38:3). Later God adds to the instruction: "Adorn yourself with majesty and dignity; clothe yourself with glory and splendor... Look on everyone who is proud and bring him low and tread down the wicked where they stand." (40:10-12).

Clearly, Job cannot play the divine warrior in full battle dress. But such a warrior does exist. There is one who is worthy.

In his Revelation, the Apostle John writes, "Then I saw heaven opened, and behold, a white horse! The one sitting on it is called Faithful and True, and in righteousness he judges and makes war. His eyes are like a flame of fire, and on his head are many diadems... And the armies of heaven, arrayed in fine linen, white and pure, were following him on white horses... He will tread the winepress of the fury of the wrath of God the Almighty." (Revelation 19:11-15).

Even as Job suffers, God is drawing up his war plans. In fact, Job's own heart is a disputed territory (2:3). The birds of prey are following the battle path, and they appear next in God's discourse. *Is it by your understanding, Job, that the hawk soars? (v. 26). Do you command the eagle to build his nest on the heights? From the eyrie on the cliffs, he spies out prey. Where the slain are, you will find the eagle; his young suck up their blood.*

The language is graphic, and also apocalyptic. When speaking of God's coming judgment, Jesus uses very similar words: "Wherever the corpse is, there the vultures will gather." (Matthew 24:28, Luke 17:37). Both Ezekiel and John describe this scavenger's feast, at the end of a cosmic battle where God delivers his people (Ezekiel 39:17-20, Revelation 19:17-18).

We are not sufficient for our ancient foe – more on him later. But there is one who fights for us. We can dress in his armor (Ephesians 6:10-18) and take courage in his victory. Hallelujah!

Interlude: Peace Donkey

That first Palm Sunday, on the threshold of Jerusalem, Jesus tells two of his disciples to appropriate a donkey. He tells the disciples exactly where to find it, and what to say if anyone asks questions. Then Jesus rides the donkey into the city (Luke 19:29-35).

As Christ approaches, the crowds shout and praise God: "Blessed is the King who comes in the name of the Lord! Peace in heaven and glory in the highest!" (Luke 19:39). The people spread leafy branches and their own cloaks on the road for Christ to ride on (Mark 11:8). Offended by what they saw as blasphemous hero-worship, the Pharisees order Jesus to rebuke his disciples, to shut down the parade. But Jesus responds, "I tell you, if these were silent, the very stones would cry out." (Luke 19:39-40).

In America, if we want to get somewhere, we drive a vehicle. The wheels we choose provide clues: are we outgoing or shy? Sensitive or macho? Conspicuous consumers, or financially struggling? Meticulously neat, or oblivious to dent and dirt?

So what did it mean that Jesus rode a donkey? We know that he has sweeter rides in his stable. When God speaks to Job, he mentions his majestic war horse, strong and fearless, bearing the weapons of battle (Job 39:19-25). Jesus is fully capable of riding such an animal, as we see in John's Revelation: "Then I saw heaven opened, and behold, a white horse! The one sitting on it is called Faithful and True, and in righteousness he judges and makes war." (Revelation 19:11).

So what does it mean that Jesus rode a donkey? This particular donkey was young and had never been ridden before (Luke 19:30). It was probably a little wild. In his discourse with Job, God also points out his wild donkey, roaming the wilderness in search of food, scorning the city and the shouts of the drivers (Job 39:5-8). Yet our Palm Sunday donkey did not act wild at all; it did not seem to mind the shouts of the people as they blessed Jesus. Jesus was able to keep the donkey perfectly calm – perhaps as great a feat as riding his war horse.

Matthew tells us that the Palm Sunday donkey was foretold by the prophet Zechariah (Matthew 21:8). Zechariah 9:9-10 reads:

Rejoice greatly, O daughter of Zion! Shout aloud, O daughter of Jerusalem!
Behold, your king is coming to you; righteous and having salvation is he,
humble and mounted on a donkey, on a colt, the foal of a donkey.
I will cut off the chariot from Ephraim, and the war horse from Jerusalem;
and the battle bow shall be cut off, and he shall speak peace to the nations;
his rule shall be from sea to sea, and from the River to the ends of the earth.

Christ rode a donkey into Jerusalem for at least two reasons. First, as a mark of humility. Donkeys are not majestic like horses; they are short and plodding, with funny ears. Even though Jesus is King of the Universe, he humbled himself to become human, humbled himself to be born into a poor family, humbled himself to live and eat with sinners. And, in the ultimate act of submission to God's will, Christ humbled himself to die on a cross (Philippians 2:6-8). "Come to me!" says Jesus, "I am gentle and lowly in heart, and you will find rest for your souls." (Matthew 11:28-30).

Second, Jesus chose the donkey as a symbol of peace. You don't ride a donkey into war. Christ was sending a message: he did not come to overthrow political regimes; his kingdom is not of this world (John 18:36). When they announced Christ's birth, the angels sang peace (Luke 2:14). By faith in Christ's sacrifice for us, we can have peace with God (Romans 5:1). We can even have peace with each other (Ephesians 2:13-19).

Surprisingly, right after his triumphal entry, Jesus wept loud tears for the people of Jerusalem. *Oh if you had only known what would give you peace!* (Luke 19:41). Despite their enthusiasm on Palm Sunday, Christ knew the Jewish people would reject the peace that he offered. Judgment Day was coming (Luke 21:22). In 70 A.D., the Romans sacked and burned Jerusalem, destroying the temple.

We have a choice, just like the people of Jerusalem. Will we run to the King on the Peace Donkey? Or will we hide, in vain, from the King on the War Horse?

Job 40:1-14 (Speechless)

Throughout the book, Job never doubts that his suffering is from the hand of God. But what kind of God would afflict his servant in this way? And what kind of relationship can Job possibly have with God now?

Over and over, Job imagines confronting God, his perceived adversary. Job's changing emotions, from despair to hope to anger, mirror our own experiences with suffering. Job asks: *How can I argue with God? He is too powerful, he would never listen, he wouldn't even let me catch my breath* (9:1-20). Job moans: *God, just leave me alone, that I may find some small happiness before I die* (10:20-21). Sometimes Job feels more courageous: *I will argue my ways to his face! Maybe, if God ties one hand behind his back, we could actually talk* (13:15, 21). Job hopes against hope: *Surely there is someone in heaven to advocate for me* (16:19, 19:25). *Surely, if I keep looking, God will allow himself to be found. God has to listen to me!* (23:1-10). And in a final act of bravado Job binds God with an oath: *Let the Almighty answer me!* (31:35).

Then, out of the whirlwind, God shows up: mightier and more marvelous than Job imagined. He is also more personal. The stars sing for joy, Sea kicks like a baby, Dawn shakes her skirts. (38:7-13). And God's concern is not just cosmic – he faithfully provides for all his creatures, even the ridiculous ostrich (39:13-18). Notably, God does not give an explanation for Job's suffering. Instead, God gives a glimpse into his own character. God's joy and love shine forth in creation; he is no sadist at all.

Then God gives Job his chance to respond. *So Job, have you found fault with my plans? Go ahead, respond to what you have heard!* (v. 2).

Job is humbled: *I am of small account, a true lightweight. I can do nothing except cover my mouth. I have nothing further to say* (vv. 4-5). This is the same man who made speech after speech, who vowed to argue his case if God would only give him the chance, who endlessly rehearsed his declarations of innocence (chs. 29, 31). Ironically, Job is speechless.

God doesn't let it go immediately; he teases Job a little bit. It's terrifying. *Dress for action like a man, Job. Answer my questions. Do you dare to condemn me, so that you can be in the right? Do you have a mighty arm like mine? Can you thunder with a voice like mine?* [cue the KA-BOOM.] (vv. 7-9).

So you don't like the way I do things? "Adorn yourself with majesty and dignity; clothe yourself with glory and splendor." *Take down the proud in your righteous anger; bury the wicked as they deserve. Then I will acknowledge your right hand can save you. You still think you can do my job, Job?* (vv. 10-14).

These are the words of the divine warrior, preparing for battle. He covers himself with light, he rides the clouds like a chariot; wind and fire are his messengers. What can we do except bless his name? (Psalm 104: 1-4). Job has complained that the wicked prosper unjustly (21:7-21). In essence, he has questioned God's sovereignty.

God wants Job to know, of course he sees the proud and wicked. He is not sitting on his hands; he has plans for their destruction. God also reminds Job that he (and we) are not in charge of the universe. We aren't qualified, and the responsibility would crush us. We can't even wear the clothes. As Job well knows, we can't even save ourselves.

When people try to play God, it's a disaster. Thankfully, God knows how to be God, and we can trust in his plan -- both for the universe, and for our own salvation.

Job 40:7-14 (Ultimate Warrior Jesus)

Job didn't like how God was running the world. And why should he? Job was a pious and faithful man, yet he lost everything. The best of all men came to the worst of all ends. And not only that, Job sees wicked people prospering, even as they oppress their fellow humans. In anguish and anger, Job demands an answer from God.

God, miraculously, appears. He gives Job (and us) a fascinating picture of what it means to be God of the universe. A joyful song pours from sky and land; God is composer, conductor, and audience. *How about you, Job? Can you carry this tune?*

But God isn't finished. The climax is coming, a great battle scene. *Job, would you like to audition for the title role? Can you even wear the gear?*

"Adorn yourself with majesty and dignity; clothe yourself with glory and splendor...
Look on everyone who is proud and bring him low and tread down the wicked where they stand...
Then will I also acknowledge to you that your own right hand can save you." (vv. 10-14).

God acknowledges that the world is not as it should be. The world is waiting for its hero, someone to take vengeance on the proud and wicked. More than that, someone who can save God's people. This hero is obviously not Job. Job couldn't save his family, he couldn't even save his own skin.

The title role of this drama belongs to Ultimate Warrior Jesus.

Isaiah prophesied about Christ, the hero of history: "Who is this... splendid in his apparel, marching in the greatness of his strength? 'It is I, speaking in righteousness, mighty to save.'" (Isaiah 63:1). According to the prophecy, on the day of vengeance and redemption, God looked around him. There was no one able to help (as even the blameless man Job realized). So what did God do? "I have trodden the winepress alone, and from the peoples no one was with me... my own arm brought me salvation, and my wrath upheld me." (Isaiah 63:3, 5). God intervened himself.

Isaiah talks about God getting ready for the great battle. "He put on righteousness as a breastplate, and a helmet of salvation on his head; he put on garments of vengeance for clothing, and wrapped himself in zeal as a cloak." (Isaiah 59:17). God, the only one who could work salvation, was ready to intercede. (Isaiah 59:16). But what did that intercession look like?

Oddly enough, it looked like suffering. Our sin had separated us from God (Isaiah 59:2). To save us, to intercede on our behalf, Christ had to bear our sin, to give himself as a sacrificial offering (Isaiah 53:10-12). He was "despised and rejected by men, a man of sorrows and acquainted with grief." (Isaiah 53:3). Christ was more righteous than Job, yet he suffered unto death – unlike Job, whose life was spared. And through his death on the cross, Christ bridged the chasm of our sin and brought us to God.

We look forward to Christ's second coming as conquering King (Revelation 19:11-16). Meanwhile, the world is still not as it should be, and the battle continues. But as people of the cross, we now have access to God's armor. We can dress in the breastplate of Christ's righteousness, we can put on the helmet of Christ's salvation – in fact, we are commanded to do so (Ephesians 6:10-18).

We are not God. We cannot create our own truth, we cannot save ourselves. But we can participate in God's salvation – both his suffering and his triumph -- through faith in the ultimate warrior hero.

Job 40:15-24 (Monsters at the End of This Book)

Behold, Behemoth! God tells Job. *I made this creature, just as I made you. And he's a Beast!*

We are nearing the end of the book of Job. God has declared his power over heaven and earth, land and sea. God has demonstrated his care for his many wild creatures. And for the climax, God wants Job to consider two monstrosities: Behemoth and Leviathan.

Some commentators take a purely naturalistic approach to this dynamic duo. They think Behemoth is some kind of hippopotamus, and Leviathan is an Egyptian crocodile. Certainly there are similarities. But as we will see, there are also important differences. Behemoth and Leviathan are frightening in a way that we cannot, should not associate with exotic zoo animals. These are creatures of mythological proportions: the monsters at the end of the book.

God does not explicitly tell Job, or us, what Behemoth and Leviathan represent. Nonetheless, we can take clues from the context. God has just alluded to a great battle, involving war horses (39:19-25) and feasting vultures (39:26-30). He has exposed the need for a divine warrior, who will bring justice to the earth (40:10-14). This begs the question, who is the opponent?

We know that Satan requested, and received, permission to afflict Job (1:6-12, 2:1-7). God does not tell Job about this discussion in the divine council. And yet, in the portraits of Behemoth and Leviathan, God gives Job a glimpse of spiritual realities. As Paul reminds us, "we do not wrestle against flesh and blood, but against the rulers, against the authorities, against the cosmic powers over this present darkness, against the spiritual forces of evil in the heavenly places." (Ephesians 6:12). In other passages of scripture, we see a dragon (Leviathan) and a beast (Behemoth) as enemies of the people of God, identified with Satan (Revelation chs. 12-13). These are terrifying forces of evil, beyond Job's comprehension. But they are not outside God's control.

So what is Behemoth like? He eats grass "like an ox," which means he is always eating. His body is strong, powerful, muscular. His tail is stiff like a cedar (several commentators note that "tail" may be a euphemism for a distinctly male organ). His bones are like iron bars. Behemoth sounds more like the brontosaurus than the hippo. God calls Behemoth "first of the works of God," an ancient and awe-inspiring creature (v. 19). Yet Behemoth is still subject to his creator – and only his creator. "Let him who made him bring near his sword!" (v. 19).

God continues: *The mountains – where the wild beasts play – yield food for him* (v. 20). It almost sounds like the mountain kingdoms are bringing Behemoth tribute. Meanwhile, Behemoth floats in the marsh, under the shade of the reeds and lotus trees (vv. 21-22). Lurking in the shadows, he is a menacing presence.

Even when the river becomes turbulent, even though the Jordan rushes against his mouth, Behemoth remains confident (v. 23). Behemoth eats, and drinks, and fears nothing. Who will capture Behemoth? "Can one take him by his eyes, or pierce his nose with a snare?" (v. 24). The question is preposterous, at least when posed to poor, sick Job.

Yet Behemoth is not God, only a creature. His maker is capable of capturing him, and slaying him if necessary. No dark forces will prevail against the divine warrior, or against those who wear Christ's armor.

Job 41:1-11 (How to Train Your Dragon -- NOT)

From ancient times, dragons have captured our imagination. Think about the mythical dragon of the Chinese zodiac; the legend of St. George; or Tolkien's Smaug. And, of course, you can trust Disney to turn fearsome beast into comic animation.

The book of Job also features a dragon, named Leviathan. God describes Leviathan for us in chapter 41. And no, this is not the Disney version for children.

So, Job, you want to go fishing for Leviathan? And what would you do if you actually caught him? I hope you have a strong hook! Do you think Leviathan will beg for you? Will he serve you loyally, a "man's best friend"? Could your girls keep him as a pet, do you think? Or maybe you want to sell him to the traders -- how will you divide him? "Lay your hands on him; remember the battle – you will not do it again!" (vv. 1-8).

Interestingly, this is not the first time Leviathan is mentioned in the book of Job. We get a glimpse, a foreshadowing, at the beginning of the story. Job has suffered his multiple disasters, and his friends have come to mourn with him. After seven days of silence, Job finally opens his mouth and curses the day of his birth. "Let the day perish on which I was born!" says Job.

"Let those curse it who curse the day,
who are ready to rouse up Leviathan.
Let the stars of its dawn be dark;
let it hope for light, but have none,
nor see the eyelids of the morning,
because it did not shut the doors of my mother's womb,
nor hide trouble from my eyes." (3:8-10)

When God created the world, he said, "Let there be light!" (Genesis 1:3). But in his pain Job calls for de-creation, a darkening of the sun and stars. To accomplish this, Job calls on the day-cursers, practitioners of the dark arts, ready to wake Leviathan. Here Leviathan plays the role of chaos monster, capable of gobbling up Job's story before it begins. We see a similar image in Revelation 12, where a great red dragon stands ready to devour the Christ child at the moment of birth (Revelation 12:4).

And this is what Job asks for, pleads for! *Erase history,* he begs. *Let me know the peaceful rest of a stillborn child* (3:16-17). God, in his wisdom, denies Job's request. But he does bring up Leviathan for Job's instruction. *What are you thinking, Job? No man has the courage to stir up Leviathan* (v.10).

If we think about it, who is Job really challenging? Who is the true author of Job's personal history? It has to be Job's creator, God. And if Job can't face Leviathan, how will he face God? (v. 10). "Who has first given to me, that I should repay him? Whatever is under the whole earth is mine." (v. 11).

Job's friends think of God's providence as a business transaction. If we are good, do all the right things, then God is obligated to bless us. If we do evil, well then, we can't complain about the consequences. But God tells Job, "That's not how it works." God owns everything already, the cattle on a thousand hills (Psalm 50:10-11). God is worthy of our loyalty, but he doesn't need our sacrifices (Mark 12:33).

Job was correct when he said, "The Lord gave and the Lord has taken away; blessed be the name of the Lord." (Job 1:21). But he was wrong to seek peace in darkness. Leviathan is not man's friend.

Job 41:12-34 (Leviathan Up Close and Personal)

God continues his description of the Leviathan, monstrous metaphor for "that ancient serpent, who is called the devil and Satan, the deceiver of the whole world." (Revelation 12:9). We remember the Satan who challenged God's protection of Job, the Satan who destroyed Job's possessions, family and health (1:6-12, 2:1-7). Not only did Satan rob Job of everything he held dear, he did so in order to foul Job's relationship with God, to show Job's faith as false. This is the hidden foe that Job has faithfully resisted, albeit with tears and anguish.

And now, God parades the Leviathan before Job. *Take a good look, up close and personal. His limbs are mighty, his frame is solid. Who is able to strip off his outer garment? Who dares come near him with a bridle? Can you make him open his mouth and say "ah"? His teeth are set in terror* (vv. 12-14).

His back is a coat of armor, rows of shields that not even air can penetrate. There is no weak link, no vulnerable spot. And for offense, this dragon sneezes fire. Flames leap from his mouth, and smoke boils from his nostrils. The forces of terror dance before him (vv. 15-22).

His neck is strong and stubborn. His flesh is firm, he has a heart of stone. He is not moved by force or persuasion. When he rises up, even the mighty angels are afraid. He is impervious to sword, spear, dart, javelin. To him, iron is like straw and bronze is like rotten wood. Arrows, sling stones, clubs – all stubble. Leviathan laughs and stands his ground (vv. 22-29).

And forget looking for a soft underbelly! Sharp shards cover his underparts, as he spreads and thrashes in the mire. The sea boils as Leviathan returns to the abyss; he leaves a white, shining wake behind him. On earth he has no equal. He is the apex predator, he has no fear. (vv. 30-33). "He sees everything that is high; he is king over all the sons of pride." (v. 34).

Talk about frightening! We can barely imagine the power of Leviathan, much less hope to defeat him. What can poor Job do, especially in his weakened state?

Perhaps one key is in the final, descriptive line: Leviathan is ruler of the sons of pride. To escape Leviathan's clutches, we must turn from pride. And in that endeavor, affliction is our friend. Suffering humbles us, forces us to recognize that our enemy is too mighty for us (Ps. 18:17), moves us to call on God alone for salvation.

Leviathan has no equal on earth (v. 33), but he is still God's creature. Everything under the whole heavens belongs to God, including Behemoth and Leviathan (40:15, 41:10-11). And though these beasts are fierce, God is fiercer still. Leviathan isn't the only one who breathes fire. Listen to God's response when David called to him for help:

"Then the earth reeled and rocked;
the foundations also of the mountains trembled and quaked,
because he was angry.
Smoke went up from his nostrils, and devouring fire from his mouth;
glowing coals flamed from him.
He bowed the heavens and came down..." (Psalm 18:7-9).

Leviathan was conquered by the blood of Christ at the cross (Rev. 12:11), and he will be defeated forever at Christ's second coming (Rev. 20:10). His sons of pride will never inherit the earth.

Interlude: Love and the Leviathan

At the climax of the book of Job, we meet two terrifying monsters. God describes the brute strength of Behemoth, fearless even as the mighty River Jordan rushes against his mouth. (Job 40:23). Next comes Leviathan, covered in plate armor "shut up closely as with a seal," and sneezing out flashes of fire (Job 41:15, 18-19). Behemoth and Leviathan represent the demonic forces of evil and chaos, against which Job and his fellow humans are powerless.

No one is so fierce, says God, that he dares to stir up Leviathan (Job 41:10). Leviathan is not a pet you can train on a leash (Job 41:5). This is a veiled rebuke of Job, who in his suffering wished for the dark forces to swallow up the day of his birth (Job 3:8). God alone has power to control the forces of evil - and to demolish them once they have served his purposes. Thus God declares his ownership over "whatever is under the whole heaven" - including Behemoth and Leviathan (Job 41:11).

We cannot manipulate God, or purchase a protection plan from earthly suffering. "Who has first given to me, that I should repay him?" asks the Lord (Job 41:11). God in his sovereignty limits evil as he sees fit. This means that God is even more terrifying - even more to be feared - than the Leviathan. (Job 41:10).

Thankfully, this is not the end of the story. God is all-powerful, but he is also love. As the Apostle John tells us, God's perfect love casts out fear. (1 John 16-19). The Old Testament wisdom literature - a canon that includes Job - gives us a picture of this love. Just as Behemoth and Leviathan are the mascots of cosmic evil and destruction, King Solomon and his bride are the mascots of cosmic love.

The Song of Solomon - an erotic wedding poem - contains the following passage, which may be familiar:

Set me as a seal upon your heart, as a seal upon your arm,
for love is as strong as death, jealousy is fierce as the grave.
Its flashes are flashes of fire, the very flame of the Lord.
Many waters cannot quench love, neither can floods drown it.
If a man offered for love all the wealth of his house, he would be utterly despised.
(SoS 8:6-7).

The parallels between Love and the two chaos monsters are striking. The forces of darkness are strong, but so is love - "as strong as death" (SoS 8:6). Rows of shields form a seal along the back of Leviathan (Job 41:15), while love is a seal on the heart and arm of the beloved (Sos 8:6). Behemoth is not afraid of drowning (Job 41:23), and neither is love, which cannot be quenched by many waters (SoS 8:7). Love even breathes out flashes of fire, just like Leviathan! (SoS 8:6, Job 41:15, 18-19).

In the face of these cosmic realities, both evil and good, worldly wealth fades in value. The book of Job delineates, in horrific detail, how riches cannot save us from destruction. All of Job's thousands of sheep and camels, his hundreds of oxen and donkeys, his very many servants, could not save him from bandits, fire, whirlwind, or skin disease (Job 1:1 - 2:8). You can't bribe God to change your lot in life (Job 41:11).

Interestingly, love also cannot be bought. Even if a man offers all the wealth of his house, his love may remain unrequited; he may find disdain instead (SoS 8:7). Who knows what brings a man and a woman together, what physical and metaphysical formulations draw two hearts to become one? The way of a man wooing a maiden is one of the wonders of the world (Proverbs 30:19).

The Song of Solomon contains an interesting admonition: "I adjure you, O daughters of Jerusalem, that you not stir up or awaken love until it pleases." (SoS 8:4). Like the Leviathan, love is a deep, cosmic force. Love is not a plaything, not a pet you can train on a leash. The consummation of marital love results in new life, i.e., babies. What Job wished Leviathan would destroy – the day of his birth – was a miracle created by the love of his parents. As God tells Job, no one should dare stir up Leviathan (Job 41:10). We should also have referent fear when stirring up romantic love.

Not all mysterious forces are evil, not by a long shot. Perfect love casts out Leviathan, both now and for eternity. And so we look forward to the final wedding feast, where God himself will wipe away every tear (Rev. 19:9, 21:4).

Job 42:1-3 (Submission)

God has finished speaking. It's time for Job's response. Now that Job finally has his audience with God, what will Job say? As we have seen before (40:4-5), Job's planned, self-justifying speeches fail him. Instead, Job concedes God's authority and cries "uncle."

"I know that you can do all things, and that no purpose of yours can be thwarted." (v. 2). Job acknowledges that God is sovereign. God can do all things – his power is not bent by human schemes or desires. God has his own designs that will not fail. And, after passing through many levels of grief and anger, Job is now ready to submit to God's will.

During the Christmas season we remember another story of submission, the story of the virgin Mary. Out of nowhere, the angel Gabriel appears and tells Mary that she is highly favored by God. "And behold, you will conceive in your womb and bear a son, and you shall call his name Jesus." (Luke 1:31).

This unplanned pregnancy would have raised many problems for Mary, especially in traditional Jewish society. What would her family say? What would her fiancé Joseph say? Would she and the baby be cast out, forced to fend for themselves, doomed to a life of poverty? Is this how God shows his "favor?" (Think about how God showed his "favor" to Job!)

But Mary's first question is pragmatic: "How will this be, since I am a virgin?" (Luke 1:34). With echoes of Job, Gabriel replies, "nothing will be impossible with God." (Luke 1:37). God is sending a Savior to redeem the world. And God can do all things to accomplish his will, even create new life in a virgin. No purpose of God's can be thwarted.

"Behold, I am the servant of the Lord," says Mary, "Let it be to me according to your word." Mary, like Job, is God's servant (Job 1:8). Yet Mary comes to the place of submission much faster, and more easily. *Yes, Lord,* says Mary. *You have spoken, let it be.*

God's grand design is beyond Mary's comprehension, yet she still accepts his authority. And so, eventually, does Job. Note that Job's understanding is also incomplete. God never told Job about his discussions with Satan in the divine council, never revealed any clues about Job's specific situation. Instead, God pointed Job's attention to the mysteries of the natural and supernatural world. And this was sufficient to bring Job to his senses.

Job acknowledges God's rebuke: Job had spoken without knowledge, thereby obscuring the word of God (Job 38:2, 42:3). Job admits, "I have uttered what I did not understand, things too wonderful for me, which I did not know." (42:3). Job knew only the immediacy of his pain – his dead children, his stolen livestock, his loathsome skin disease. Job did not stop to think about God's care for the larger creation, and where his small story might fit. He did not consider what hidden forces might lurk beyond human perception. Yet at the end of it all, when God graciously gives Job a glimpse of the big picture, Job calls it "too wonderful for me."

Have you been fighting God, trying to understand why he has allowed some suffering into your life? Bad things happen, and God's plan seems incomprehensible to us. Nonetheless, as we crawl through fog, we can find, with Job and Mary, that place of submission. We can trust that God has a good plan, a plan that will someday make glorious sense of our current afflictions (Romans 8:18, 28).

Job 42:4-6 (Repentance)

In his most bitter moments, Job seeks God. "Oh, that I knew where I might find him, that I might come even to his seat!" (23:2-3). But what was Job's motive? He wanted to argue his case; he wanted God to acknowledge the fact that Job, an innocent man, had been wronged (23:4-7). As we have seen, God responded to Job's demand for an audience. But instead of Job questioning God, God questions him (38:3).

Twice during their encounter, God pauses and allows Job a response. The first time, Job states he has no words; he is speechless (40:4-5). The second time, Job issues a retraction of his challenge. *I didn't understand*, says Job (42:3). *I know now, it was not my place to question you, Lord* (42:4).

Job concludes:

"I had heard of you by the hearing of the ear, but now my eye sees you;

therefore I despise myself, and repent in dust and ashes." (42:5-6)

In the past, Job knew something about God. He knew enough to worship God, and to turn from evil. In fact, God acknowledged Job as his "servant" (Job 1:1, 5, 8). But then Job was plunged into suffering. In his anguish, Job accused God of being arbitrary, of acting as his enemy (9:22-24, 16:6-17). Job's sense of estrangement from God intensified his pain. His understanding of God was inadequate in the face of his afflictions.

Instead of the confrontation that Job desired, God offers communion. He gives Job a more complete picture of himself: his joyful work as the creator and caretaker of the universe (chs. 38-39), his power over the forces of darkness in the world (chs. 40-41). If we saw the fullness of God's glory, our puny human brains would explode (Exodus 33:20). Nonetheless, God opens Job's eyes and reveals himself in a supernatural way.

And Job changes. Note that his knowledge of his own situation has not changed. He has no idea that Satan directly instigated his suffering. He has no idea that God called him "blameless" from the very beginning – thus drawing Satan's attention. Instead, Job relinquishes his demand to know these things.

Before, Job hated his life (7:16, 10:1). Now, after seeing God, Job despises his sin. By accusing God of wrongdoing, Job was setting himself above God. He was at risk of becoming a "son of pride," estranged from wisdom and aligned with the forces of evil (28:7-8, 41:34). As Elihu noted, one of the functions of suffering is repentance and growth: God "delivers the afflicted by their affliction, and opens their ear by adversity." (36:15). After his long road of suffering, Job not only sees God, he sees himself clearly as well. And Job responds in humble repentance, in dust and ashes.

God does not leave Job in the dust. Instead, God rebukes the three friends, Eliphaz, Bildad and Zophar: "My anger burns against you [Eliphaz] and against your two friends, for you have not spoken of me what is right, as my servant Job has." (41:7). While Job had much to learn, his heart continually desired a right relationship with God (29:1-5). In contrast, Job's friends treated God as a business partner; they were interested only in God's blessings, and not God himself. Their pat answers and rigid theology contributed to Job's suffering, under the guise of comfort (21:34).

As God praises Job and expresses displeasure with Job's friends, Job receives his long-awaited vindication.

Job 42:7-9 (Three Fools)

When news of Job's calamity reached Eliphaz, Bildad, and
Zophar, they made plans for a reunion. Each man traveled from his
own place, then set out together to visit Job. Their road trip was for
sympathy, not pleasure. The friends were truly grieved – crying out,
sitting in the dust, and commiserating with Job in silence for seven
days (2:11-13). The time, effort, and expense of their journey
meant nothing when compared with Job's losses.

But then they opened their mouths. They tried to be
encouraging, at first. But Job was so distraught, so stubborn, so
unorthodox in his views, that the friends became frustrated. They
called Job a babbling windbag, a stupid jackass, a crafty sinner who
deserved to be terrorized (8:2, 11:3, 12, 15:1-6, 18:8-21, 20:5-29,
22:5-11). Why would Job's friends say such things? After all, Job
was a great man, well-known for his integrity (1:1-3).

Perhaps this is just the fickle nature of human beings. During
his earthly ministry, Jesus was no stranger to false friends. The
crowds sang his praises, then demanded his crucifixion. In five
short days, Palm Sunday became Good Friday. Judas the disciple
became Judas the betrayer.

Or perhaps the friends were experiencing compassion fatigue.
Could you sit with a bereaved friend for seven days straight? Just
how many hours were they supposed to listen, while Job cursed the
day he was born? After all, they had their own lives to get back to.
When was Job going to get over himself?

Or perhaps the three friends felt scared, threatened by Job's
situation. Eliphaz wonders, when has a truly innocent person ever
perished? (4:7). If a man does what is right, God is obligated to
help him. If catastrophe comes, someone must have sinned. Yet
Job, after suffering massive tragedy, staunchly maintained his
innocence. The implications are unthinkable. You mean God can
do anything he wants, even allow his faithful servant to suffer?

The sovereignty of God leaps from every page of the Bible. We love to quote Jeremiah 29:11: God has good plans for us! Or how about, God causes all things to work together for good! (Romans 8:28). But what if those plans include tribulation, or distress, or persecution, or famine, or nakedness, or danger, or sword? (Romans 8:35). What if those plans include chronic illness, a broken family, and job disappointment? Or in Job's case, what if those plans include total destruction of everything and everyone he holds dear, down to his very own skin?

In chapter after chapter, Job shouted his sadness, his anger, his outrage. His friends responded with the same old formula: God wouldn't do that to an innocent person. Then God appears. *I can do anything,* God says. *My power is unlimited, and so is my love.* Job is overwhelmed, falling before God in repentance.

Then God says to the three friends, "My anger burns against you... for you have not spoken of me what is right, as my servant Job has." (v. 7). God instructs the three friends to prepare a large sacrifice, seven bulls and seven rams, and have Job pray for them. Job, the suffering servant, will become priest to his three foolish friends. "I will accept his prayer not to deal with you according to your folly. For you have not spoken of me what is right, as my servant Job has." (v. 8).

Because of Job's intercession, God forgives the three friends. And (it is implied) Job forgives them as well. Job's journey of suffering has led to insight and reconciliation, which he shares with his friends.

Job 42:10-16 (Happily Ever After)

While Job was suffering, his friends assumed he must have done something awful to deserve it. But now, Job is vindicated! God declares Job righteous in front of his friends (vv. 7-8). Job's relationship with God, and his relationships with his friends, have been restored.

In his time of trial, Job was an outcast, estranged from his family and the larger society. Job's cries were pitiful: *My friends have forgotten me. I am a stench to my own brothers and sisters. Hoodlums spit at me and mock me. Have mercy!* (19:13-19; 30:1-15). But now Job's trial is over. His family and friends came to his home and eat with him, a sign of renewed fellowship. They show him the sympathy and comfort that he was craving. And they each gave him "a piece of money and a ring of gold," seed capital so Job can start over. (v. 11).

With the favor of his friends, God restores Job's fortunes as well. "The Lord gave Job twice as much as he had before." (v.10). God is not stingy when it comes to the restoration business. Sheep, camels, oxen, female donkeys – all doubled. Job was a great man before his time of affliction, but "the Lord blessed the latter days of Job more than his beginning." (v. 12).

Job is also blessed with seven sons and three daughters, the same as before his troubles. (1:2, 42:13). These seven sons, and ten children overall, signify a perfect, complete cohort. We don't know how God worked this blessing in Job's life. Perhaps Job took a second wife, to replace his first wife who told him to curse God and die (2:9). Or perhaps God graciously allowed the couple to continue to have children into their old age. God has certainly done this before – think Sarah and Abraham, or Elizabeth and Zechariah.

As we have seen, there are many similarities between the innocent suffering of Job, and the sufferings of Christ our Messiah. Here we have one final parallel: God did not abandon his suffering servant. As Isaiah prophesied, "he shall see his offspring; he shall prolong his days." (Isaiah 54:10). This is exactly what happened with Job. He lived 140 more years, and got to see his great-grandchildren. If 70 years is a full lifespan (Psalm 90:10), then Job lived a double-portion, starting after his period of trial.

The emphasis on Job's daughters is interesting. We learn their names – Jemimah, Keziah, and Keren-happuch – and the fact they are extremely beautiful. Their names appear to accentuate their beauty. Jemimah means day or dove, alluding to the return of light and peace. Keziah is an aromatic spice like cinnamon, and Keren-happuch means horn of Kohl, a cosmetic. Job cherishes these beautiful women, with their lovely names, and gives them an inheritance with their brothers. (vv. 14-15).

I am struck by Job's attitude toward his children before and after his time of affliction. In chapter one, Job is very concerned about his children's behavior. "Perhaps they have sinned," he thinks, and he offers sacrifices on their behalf. Those of us with prodigal children can relate to Job's anxieties. How tragic that Job's children all died despite his prayers!

But by the end of the story, Job has changed. It seems he is able to relax and enjoy his children for who they are, especially his beautiful daughters with their pleasant, almost frivolous names. Job is no longer plagued with anxiety over whether God will favor them. Strangely, Job's extended suffering – and his confrontation with God's absolute sovereignty -- allow him to be fully present. I imagine Job with happy tears as he savors the renewal God has brought into his life.

Conclusion: The Passion of Job

As we come near the end, you may wonder about the title of this book, "The Passion of Job." "Passion" comes from a Latin word meaning suffering or enduring. Christians use the term to describe the week between Palm Sunday and Good Friday, where Christ entered Jerusalem in triumph only to suffer a shameful death on the cross.

As we have seen, there are parallels between the suffering of Job and the suffering of Christ.

Both Job and Christ are described as righteous.

The story of Job opens with God bragging on Job: "a blameless and upright man, who fears God and turns away from evil." (Job 1:8). Job brags on himself quite a bit also, as we have seen in chapter 31. In this fallen world, Job is as good as they come, "none like him on earth." Yet not even Job is perfect. He feels guilt over the sins of his youth, and he suspects he may have hidden sins as well. (Job 13:23, 26). At the climax of the story, when Job sees God face to face, he bows to the ground in repentance (Job 40:4-5, 42:2-6). Nonetheless, God remains pleased with Job, calling him "my servant" (Job 42:7).

Of course, Jesus took righteousness to a whole new level. Like Job, Jesus is described as God's servant. Unlike Job, Jesus was also God's beloved Son (Luke 9:35). Jesus was tempted dreadfully, even by the devil himself; yet Jesus never sinned, not even once (Hebrews 4:15). While Job was righteous in relative terms, Jesus was righteous in absolute terms, free from all sin and deceit (2 Corinthians 5:21; 1 Peter 2:22). John, who was Christ's best friend on earth, described him as "Jesus Christ the Righteous." (1 John 2:1).

Both Job and Christ suffered unjustly.

The Bible makes clear that Job did not do anything to deserve the devastation he experienced. Job's three friends try to draw a straight line from some hidden sin in Job's life to the suffering he experienced. Yet the biblical story does not permit such line-drawing.

Christ also suffered as an innocent man. Pontius Pilate, who ordered the crucifixion under pressure from the crowds, stated "I find no guilt in him." (John 19:6). And the Roman centurion guarding the cross marveled, "Certainly this man was innocent." (Luke 23:47).

Both Job and Christ suffered physical pain and rejection.

Not only did Job lose everything, he suffered intense physical pain. His blackened skin, full of sores, disfigured him beyond recognition. His pain would not let him sleep (Job 30:16-18, 27-30). Before his death, Christ also endured horrible bodily pain: flogging, a crown of thorns, and the torture of crucifixion itself. (Mark 15:15-25).

But physical pain is not the only kind, and many times not the worst. Job was accused by his friends, scorned and mocked. "Men have gaped at me with their mouth; they have struck me insolently on the cheek; they mass themselves together against me." (Job 16:10-11, Job 30:1-15). Job's lament seems almost prophetic: Christ likewise faced mocking and betrayal, both from the crowds and from his close friends, Judas and Peter. (Luke 22:47-65).

But here is a key difference between the passion of Job and that of Christ: God preserved Job's life and did not allow Satan to kill him. In contrast, God did not spare the life of his beloved Son, but sent Jesus to his death.

Job only thought that God had rejected him. But Christ was, in fact, rejected and abandoned by God as he took on our sin at the cross. Thus his cry, "My God, my God, why have you forsaken me?" (Matthew 27:46). Thankfully, that was not the end of the story.

Both Job and Christ were fighting a spiritual battle.

Job's suffering had a hidden spiritual component. In the opening scenes, Satan questioned Job's loyalty to God, and God allowed Satan to test Job. But Job did not know that he was the subject of a heavenly wager. And Job certainly did not submit to God's plan for his life. In his speeches, Job curses the day of his birth, accuses God of acting capriciously, and demands that God appear and explain himself. Job is not a happy camper; in fact, he hated his life.

Christ was engaged in an even greater contest, for the fate of the world itself. Could the sting of death be defeated? Could mankind be redeemed back into God's family?

Here we see another key difference between Job and Christ. Christ knew what the agony of the cross would entail, body and soul. In the Garden of Gethsemane, he fell to the ground and sweat great drops of blood. Yet his prayer was, "Nevertheless, not my will, but yours, be done." (Luke 22:41-44). Christ suffered knowingly and willingly; he was obedient to God's will.

Both Job and Christ were restored.

God restored Job's fortunes, blessing him with double the wealth, a full house of children, and many happy years (Job 42:10-17). This lengthy tale of woe, at last, has a happy ending.

Even more miraculously, that very first Easter Sunday, God raised Jesus from the dead (Luke 24). And the restoration did not stop there. Because of Christ's obedience to death, "God has highly exalted him and bestowed on him the name that is above every name, so that at the name of Jesus every knee should bow, in heaven and on earth and under the earth, and every tongue confess that Jesus Christ is Lord, to the glory of God the Father." (Philippians 2:9-11). We who believe in Christ look forward to a future restoration of the entire world (Romans 8:18-25).

Job interceded for his friends, but Christ saves even his former enemies.

As the book of Job concludes, God rebukes Job's friends for speaking improperly. God then instructs the friends to make sacrifices and have Job pray for them (Job 42:7-9). Job the righteous, who suffered, was able to intercede for his friends and save them from God's anger.

Yet again, we see Christ is the better intercessor. Christ is at God's right hand praying for us eternally. (Hebrews 7:25, Romans 8:34). Since the time of Job, Satan has been the accuser, pointing out our sins; yet Christ is the great Redeemer who reconciles us to God. And he saves us even though we were enemies of God and spiritually dead (Romans 5:8-10).

Whatever your sufferings may be, I pray the Holy Spirit comforts you with the words of Job, who hated his life, and Christ, who gave his life for you.